NOAH

ANOTHER STORM IS COMING

E.G. WHITE

Remnant
Publications

NOAH

ANOTHER STORM IS COMING

Remnant Publications, Inc., Coldwater, Michigan

Printed in the United States of America

ISBN 978-1-629130-17-0

Cover and interior design by Remnant Publications, Inc., Coldwater, Michigan

Compiled from the original works of E. G. White: *Patriarchs and Prophets, The Desire of Ages,* and *The Great Controversy*

Another Storm Is Coming

And as it was in the days of Noah, so it will be also in the days of the Son of Man: They ate, they drank, they married wives, they were given in marriage, until the day that Noah entered the ark, and the flood came and destroyed them all. Likewise as it was also in the days of Lot: They ate, they drank, they bought, they sold, they planted, they built; but on the day that Lot went out of Sodom it rained fire and brimstone from heaven and destroyed them all.

—Luke 17:26–29 NKJV

Table *of* Contents

Part 2: The Coming Storm

"As in the Days of Lot..."

Part 3: The Problem of Evil

"As On that Day..."

Introduction

From the Publishers

In every age, there have always been people who had a global vision. They envisioned a world of peace, progress, and prosperity. However, history also testifies that in these moments of great optimism, individuals arose who challenged this vision. Individuals who predicted a different future. Indeed, these conflicts of vision serve as the story within history. This idea is particularly clear in the biblical story of Noah.

The story of Noah reveals two types of visions. One in which we strive to create what we *want to see,* and the other in which we strive to prepare ourselves for what we *will see.* One is uncertain, the other is certain. One is humanly based, the other is divinely based.

When the people of Noah's day looked upon the earth, they saw no cloud on the horizon. Yes, there were issues of violence and corruption, but it seemed that things would go on and get better. However, Noah saw something else, for God had warned him of a coming flood to destroy the earth.

Thus, Noah saw a planet rapidly plummeting to its destruction. But this vision did not render him sarcastic or cynical. Nor did it paralyze him to inactivity. The impending doom moved Noah to the greatest work of his life. A work that he would surely have to defend, as God had spoken to him alone.

Indomitable Faith

Noah's story speaks of a faith common only to the greatest world changers of time. A faith that believed even when… everything else said doubt. A faith that believed in the darkness what it had always known in the light. A faith that believed even in severe delay. A faith that marathoned years of criticism and accusations of lunacy. A faith that makes the onlooker wonder, "How could one man believe so long against so many odds?"

Not only does this patriarch's experience bid us to an indomitable faith, but also to do it, if necessary, alone. The halls of time bear the image of those who had the courage of their convictions. Those who, like Noah, were willing to build arks before one drop of rain had ever fallen.

Often times, we stop at making metaphors from the past in order to speak to the present. We do not well to do so. For when the conditions in the days of Noah are more closely examined, we find Noah not to be an instructive fable or moving myth, but a vision of our own time:

- A time in which revelations from God, such as the Bible, are questioned with an unrelenting skepticism, and anyone who purports to believe them suffers accusations of mental illness or delusion.
- A time when gross evils and injustices are legislated and even intellectually defended by academics under the guise of scholarship.
- A time when having an opinion or a moral standard sits under the title of "judgmental" or "lambasted" as "outmoded."
- A time when society cries out for swift justice or unforgivingness against particular crimes, while it embraces an entrenched legal system whose loopholes allow brazen criminals to obtain mercy because of a technicality—instead of sincere sorrow for their actions.

The parallels to our day take us beyond present-day reflections to *a gathering storm*. A coming storm that serves as portentous signs of a global destruction. On the authority of God's Word, the author of this book aptly describes this storm elsewhere thus:

"The conditions in the great cities proclaim in thunder tones that the hour of God's judgment is come and that the end of all things earthly is at hand. In quick succession the judgments of God will follow one another—fire, and flood, and earthquake, with war and bloodshed. The angel of mercy cannot much longer shelter the impenitent. The storm is gathering; and those only will stand who respond to the invitations of mercy." (From Splendor to Shadow, 150)

"By the word of God ... the world that then existed perished, being flooded with water. But the heavens and the earth which are now preserved by the same word, are reserved for fire until the day of judgment and perdition of ungodly men" (2 Peter 3:5–7 NKJV). In connection with this biblical passage, the author of this present book on Noah states: "*Another storm is coming*. The earth will again be swept by the desolating wrath of God, and sin and sinners will be destroyed" (p. 40 from chapter 2 of this book, under the subtitle "ANOTHER STORM IS COMING").

The Heart of This Book

Noah's experience allows us to vouchsafe a glimpse into heaven's response to such an earthly predicament. Heaven is not blind to the aches of the human heart nor will it remain silent. Heaven grants a time of probation, but not forever.

A greater justice is soon to dawn upon a world gone mad. A justice that spares no sentient soul of any culture. Planetary in its scope, such a destruction should command the attention of every nation and every mind. But this justice serves as a harbinger of an even greater mercy—and grace.

While many question today, as perhaps they did in the days of Noah, why God would allow such a world to continue so long with no heavenly response, they fail to see the patience, love, and mercy that the length of time reveals. It will be manifest, as in the days of Noah, that God's heart is always reluctant to bring catastrophe upon the families of the earth.

This is really the essence of the matter: God's heart.

Why does God have the right to destroy the world? How can we be sure that His destruction is just and appropriate? If there is such a being as God, what is He like and can we know Him? Noah's experience touches these timeless themes and questions that have encumbered the memorable works of literature, film, art, philosophy, and theology.

The age-old concern regarding the origin of evil and human suffering saturates the story of Noah. Suffering visits every home and life, but how can we find meaning in the midst of our pain? Yet one can only wonder if the experience of Noah is but another chapter in a greater narrative—the real story—a controversy that dates back before our world began, and how this story will soon end. Perhaps there are greater realities beyond our human perceptions at work. Perhaps our day is not just another chapter in some meta-narrative of the cosmos, but the final chapter. Who then will be the "Noah" in this chapter?

Why This Book on Noah?

Both Jesus and the apostles spoke about the historicity and universality of the Flood.

Often, the biblical account of Noah has been reserved for either the shelves of doctors' and dentists' offices or simply a didactic tool to teach children lessons of faith, endurance, judgment, and the power of God. However, the biblical account of Noah and the Flood in Genesis 6–9, makes claims about history whose implications no serious thinker can ignore.

More than half a century ago, Christian theologian, Dr. Alfred M. Rehwinkel, summed up the implications in his book (1960), p. xv:

"Next to Creation, the Flood of Noah's time is the greatest event in the history of our earth. Nothing comparable with it has happened since nor will happen until the final destruction of this universe in the fire of Judgment Day. The Flood marks the end of a world of transcendent beauty, created by God as a perfect abode for man, and the beginning of a new world, a mere shadowy replica of its original glory. In all recorded history there is no other event except the Fall which has had such a revolutionary effect upon the topography and condition of this earth which has so profoundly affected human history and every phase of life as it now exists in its manifold forms in the world. No geologist, biologist, or student of history can afford to ignore this great catastrophe."

These implications of the Flood in Noah's day have spawned considerable debate for quite some time. Some dismiss the event as a mere story—in the sense of a legend or myth, or an exaggeration of a local flood story. But others, believers throughout the centuries, have always maintained that the Flood account is veritable and historical. They have believed it to be a *real* story that holds the keys to crucial questions about the nature of God, the future of our world, and the origin and end of evil.

The Flood is a story God wants to be told. It occupies more than a third of the first eleven chapters of Genesis—chapters that chronicle the first 2000 years of earth's history. More chapters are devoted to the Flood of Noah's day than even the Creation record.

Indeed, the credibility of the canon of Scripture, and even that of Jesus, are seriously challenged if the veracity of the global Flood (or Deluge) in Noah's day is denied. And to trivialize or undermine the story of Noah builds a segue way to an ultimate denial of faith.

Both Jesus and the apostles spoke about the historicity and universality of the Flood. And they both saw encapsulated in the Flood account an insight into the future of a world—a world that would rekindle the flames of unbridled passions and be so stupefied by pleasure that it would not even sense the tsunami approaching as it sits on the sands of time.

As in the days of Noah, the storm is gathering again!

The Author of This Book

E.G. White (1827–1915) wrote and lived among the most formidable vessels heaven has ever used in the not too distant church history. Christian luminaries like Dwight L. Moody, F. B. Meyer, Henry Drummond, R. A. Torrey, Charles Spurgeon, and Oswald Chambers pushed the kingdom forward through scholarship, biblical preaching, and evangelistic endeavors.

E. G. White advanced the kingdom by pen. An extraordinary woman, her genteel manner lighted upon every work she produced, which made her revolutionary ideas palatable and accessible to the common soul while refreshing the theologian with her expression and simplicity. Her pen has stirred millions into a deeper knowledge of their Savior, a broader concept of education, a more meaningful approach to health, a revived appreciation of the power of the home, and to a style of leadership that values integrity supremely.

She wrote more than 5,000 periodical articles and 40 books during her lifetime. But today—including compilations from her 50,000 pages of manuscripts—more than 120 titles are available in English. This is remarkable, considering the fact that her formal schooling ended at age 9!

She offers a rational basis for anyone to trust the truthfulness of the account, and thoughtful responses to the plethora of skeptical attacks.

E. G. White is the most translated female nonfiction writer in the entire history of literature and also the most translated America nonfiction author of either gender. Her life-changing masterpiece on Christian living, *Steps to Christ*, has been published in about 150 languages.

Her crowning literary achievement is the five-volume *Century Classics Collection*. Widely acclaimed as one of the best devotional commentaries on the entire Bible, the *Century Classics* begins and ends with the theme "God Is Love."

The contents of this present book on Noah are drawn from three of the principal works of E.G. White in the five-volume *E. G. White Century Classics Collection*. The books are *Patriarchs and Prophets, The Desire of Ages,* and *The Great Controversy.* In these works she has insightfully expounded upon the account of Noah and its relationship with the events of Lot's day, our day, and the end of time.

E. G. White lived most of her life during the nineteenth century, and as is characteristic of literary writers during that century, paragraphs and chapters tend to be long. In this present work—*Noah: Another Storm Is Coming*—the publishers have broken up long chapters and paragraphs, and where deemed necessary, have inserted subheadings and pull-out quotes in the original text of E. G. White's original material. These editorial tweaks are designed to allow for easier reading for today's contemporary audience. But none of these minor editorial helps by the publishers have altered the original text of the books from which this present volume is excerpted.

The Message of the Book

The three-fold division of this book on Noah is organized using the scriptural expressions "As in the Days of Noah," "As in the days of Lot," and "As on that day" to take us through events that cascade from the real story in the day of the patriarch, through our own day, to the day when Christ shall come. Together, they paint a clear picture of the great controversy between right and wrong, truth and error, Christ and Satan.

In Part I of this work, the author has woven together profound devotional reflections on the biblical account of the Flood in Noah's day. She offers a rational basis for anyone to trust the truthfulness of the account, and thoughtful responses to the plethora of skeptical attacks. Then she navigates the reader through the Flood's relationship to the existence of fossils, the geologic column and the conditions of the earth's surface and more. Finally she traces the origin of the different races and languages to Noah's descendants and the events associated with the Tower of Babel. The marriage of the theological and scientific in her account is desperately relevant at worst.

E. G. White's humility seems to color every one of her written works. And this book is no exception. While she gives due diligence to that which can be known and understood by scientists and theologians, she also urges thinkers to tread softly. Such an attitude is not a crutch for a lack of intellect, but an honest dealing in terms of the limitation of man, as God not only employed natural means but also supernatural means in the destruction of the world by flood. Natural we can explain, supernatural we cannot.

The depth of her insight shines even more in Part II. Here, she draws the parallels between the Flood and the fiery demise of Sodom and Gomorrah. Thus, we have allowed her to further develop these subtle hints in her chapters on the Flood in a section entitled, "As in the Days of Lot." Masterfully, she builds a case for how God can maintain His claim as beneficent and eternally loving alongside His justice in the days of Noah and Lot.

Though we refer more to the destructive portions of these accounts, the author does not let us leave with a gloom and doom picture. In Part III, she paints the contrast of destruction on one side and deliverance on the other. And then she peels back the fabric of our reality and takes the reader to a time and place where many of our deepest heart questions are answered by an ancient feud and mystery—or as she calls it, "the great controversy." Yet, her goal is not just understanding but hope. Hope that God will deliver us from this ominous time of trouble. Hope that one day the universe will beat with one heart and pulse of harmony.

The publishers are releasing this book—*Noah: Another Storm Is Coming*—in the hope that readers will be led to appreciate the Word of God as the guide of life, to a experience the saving knowledge of Jesus Christ, and to develop the kind of faith Noah had—an indomitable faith which is the hallmark of those who have changed their worlds.

"By faith Noah, being divinely warned of things not yet seen, moved with godly fear, prepared an ark for the saving of his household, by which he condemned the world and became heir of the righteousness which is according to faith." (Hebrews 11:7 NKJV)

Another storm is coming. Be the "Noah."

Part 1

Thought Questions

- *What were the physical and moral conditions of the world before the Flood—the antediluvian world?*
- *What message did Noah preach while building the ark, and how was it received?*
- *What actually took place during and after the Flood, and how does this help to explain the existence of fossils, certain physical conditions on the earth surface, and the occurrence of natural phenomena, such as earthquakes and volcanoes?*
- *We admire the rainbow for its beauty, yet what true purpose is it to serve?*
- *What is the relationship between the veracity of the Flood and Creation accounts and the issues of faith and science?*
- *How are questions about the origin of the different races and languages related to Noah's descendants and the events associated with the Tower of Babel?*

The Real Story

"As it was in the days of Noah ..."

And ***as it was in the days of Noah****, so it will be also in the days of the Son of Man: They ate, they drank, they married wives, they were given in marriage, until the day that Noah entered the ark, and the flood came and destroyed them all. (Luke 17:26, 27 NKJV, emphasis added)*

Knowing this first: that scoffers will come in the last days, walking according to their own lusts, and saying, 'Where is the promise of His coming? ... For this they willfully forget: that by the word of God ... the world that then existed perished, being flooded with water. But the heavens and the earth which are now preserved by the same word, are reserved for fire until the day of judgment and perdition of ungodly men. (2 Peter 3:3–7 NKJV)

Chapter 1

Based on Genesis 6 and 7.

The Building of the Ark

The Flood—Part I

In the days of Noah a double curse was resting upon the earth in consequence of Adam's transgression and of the murder committed by Cain. Yet this had not greatly changed the face of nature. There were evident tokens of decay, but the earth was still rich and beautiful in the gifts of God's providence.

The hills were crowned with majestic trees supporting the fruit-laden branches of the vine. The vast, gardenlike plains were clothed with verdure, and sweet with the fragrance of a thousand flowers. The fruits of the earth were in great variety, and almost without limit. The trees far surpassed in size, beauty, and perfect proportion any now to be found; their wood was of fine grain and hard substance, closely resembling stone, and hardly less enduring. Gold, silver, and precious stones existed in abundance.

The human race yet retained much of its early vigor. But a few generations had passed since Adam had access to the tree which was to prolong life; and man's existence was still measured by centuries. Had that long-lived people, with their rare powers to plan and execute, devoted themselves to the service of God, they would have made their Creator's name a praise in the earth, and would have answered the purpose for which He gave them life. But they failed to do this.

There were many giants, men of great stature and strength, renowned for wisdom, skillful in devising the most cunning and wonderful works; but their guilt in giving loose rein to iniquity was in proportion to their skill and mental ability.

The Antediluvian World

God bestowed upon these antediluvians many and rich gifts; but they used His bounties to glorify themselves, and turned them into a curse by fixing their affections upon the gifts instead of the Giver. They employed the gold and silver, the precious stones and the choice wood, in the construction of habitations for themselves, and endeavored to excel one another in beautifying their dwellings with the most skillful workmanship.

They sought only to gratify the desires of their own proud hearts, and reveled in scenes of pleasure and wickedness. Not desiring to retain God in their knowledge, they soon came to deny His existence. They adored nature in place of the God of nature. They glorified human genius, worshiped the works of their own hands, and taught their children to bow down to graven images.

In the green fields and under the shadow of the goodly trees they set up the altars of their idols. Extensive groves, that retained their foliage throughout the year, were dedicated to the worship of false gods. With these groves were connected beautiful gardens, their long, winding avenues overhung with fruit-bearing trees of all descriptions, adorned with statuary, and furnished with all that could delight the senses or minister to the voluptuous desires of the people, and thus allure them to participate in the idolatrous worship.

Man will rise no higher than his conceptions of truth, purity, and holiness.

Men put God out of their knowledge and worshiped the creatures of their own imagination; and as the result, they became more and more debased. The psalmist describes the effect produced upon the worshiper by the adoration of idols. He says, "They that make them are like unto them; so is every one that trusteth in them." Psalm 115:8.

It is a law of the human mind that by beholding we become changed. Man will rise no higher than his conceptions of truth, purity, and holiness. If the mind is never exalted above the level of humanity, if it is not uplifted by faith to contemplate infinite wisdom and love, the man will be constantly sinking lower and lower. The worshipers of false gods clothed their deities with human attributes and passions, and thus their standard of character was degraded to the likeness of sinful humanity. They were defiled in consequence.

"God saw that the wickedness of man was great in the earth, and that every imagination of the thoughts of his heart was only evil continually. … The earth also was corrupt before God; and the earth was filled with violence." God had given men His commandments as a rule of life, but His law was transgressed, and every conceivable sin was the result. The wickedness of men was open and daring, justice was trampled in the dust, and the cries of the oppressed reached unto heaven.

Polygamy had been early introduced, contrary to the divine arrangement at the beginning. The Lord gave to Adam one wife, showing His order in that respect. But after the Fall, men chose to follow their own sinful desires; and as the result, crime and wretchedness rapidly increased. Neither the marriage relation nor the rights of property were respected. Whoever coveted the wives or the possessions of his neighbor, took them by force, and men exulted in their deeds of violence. They delighted in destroying the life of animals; and the use of flesh for food rendered them still more cruel and bloodthirsty, until they came to regard human life with astonishing indifference.

The world was in its infancy; yet iniquity had become so deep and widespread that God could no longer bear with it; and He said, "I will destroy man whom I have created from the face of the earth."

Iniquity had become so deep and widespread that God could no longer bear with it.

He declared that His Spirit should not always strive with the guilty race. If they did not cease to pollute with their sins the world and its rich treasures, He would blot them from His creation, and would destroy the things with which He had delighted to bless them; He would sweep away the beasts of the field, and the vegetation which furnished such an abundant supply of food, and would transform the fair earth into one vast scene of desolation and ruin.

The Building of the Ark

Amid the prevailing corruption, Methuselah, Noah, and many others labored to keep alive the knowledge of the true God and to stay the tide of moral evil.

A hundred and twenty years before the Flood, the Lord by a holy angel declared to Noah His purpose, and directed him to build an ark. While building the ark he was to preach that God would bring a flood of water upon the earth to destroy the wicked. Those who would believe the message, and would prepare for that event by repentance and reformation, should find pardon and be saved. Enoch had repeated to his children what God had shown him in regard to the Flood, and Methuselah and his sons, who lived to hear the preaching of Noah, assisted in building the ark.

God gave Noah the exact dimensions of the ark and explicit directions in regard to its construction in every particular. Human wisdom could not have devised a structure of so great strength and durability. God was the designer, and Noah the master builder. It was constructed like the hull of a ship, that it might float upon the water, but in some respects it more nearly resembled a house. It was three stories high, with but one door, which was in the side. The light was admitted at the top, and the different apartments were so arranged that all were lighted. The material employed in the construction of the ark was the cypress, or gopher wood, which would be untouched by decay for hundreds of years.

The building of this immense structure was a slow and laborious process. On account of the great size of the trees and the nature of the wood, much more labor was required then than now to prepare timber, even with the greater strength which men then possessed. All that man could do was done to render the work perfect, yet the ark could not of itself have withstood the storm which was to come upon the earth. God alone could preserve His servants upon the tempestuous waters.

"By faith Noah, being warned of God of things not seen as yet, moved with fear, prepared an ark to the saving of his house; by the which he condemned the world, and became heir of the righteousness which is by faith." Hebrews 11:7. While Noah was giving his warning message to the world, his works testified of his sincerity. It was thus that his faith was perfected and made evident. He gave the world an example of believing just what God says.

All that he possessed, he invested in the ark. As he began to construct that immense boat on dry ground, multitudes came from every direction to see the strange sight and to hear the earnest, fervent words of the singular preacher. Every blow struck upon the ark was a witness to the people.

Many at first appeared to receive the warning; yet they did not turn to God with true repentance. They were unwilling to renounce their sins. During the time that elapsed before the coming of the Flood, their faith was tested, and they failed to endure the trial. Overcome by the prevailing unbelief, they finally joined their former associates in rejecting the solemn message.

Some were deeply convicted, and would have heeded the words of warning; but there were so many to jest and ridicule, that they partook of the same spirit, resisted the invitations of mercy, and were soon among the boldest and most defiant scoffers; for none are so reckless and go to such lengths in sin as do those who have once had light, but have resisted the convicting Spirit of God.

Professed Worshipers of God

The men of that generation were not all, in the fullest acceptation of the term, idolaters. Many professed to be worshipers of God. They claimed that their idols were representations of the Deity, and that through them the people could obtain a clearer conception of the divine Being. This class were foremost in rejecting the preaching of Noah. As they endeavored to represent God by material objects, their minds were blinded to His majesty and power; they ceased to realize the holiness of His character, or the sacred, unchanging nature of His requirements.

As sin became general, it appeared less and less sinful, and they finally declared that the divine law was no longer in force; that it was contrary to the character of God to punish transgression; and they denied that His judgments were to be visited upon the earth.

Had the men of that generation obeyed the divine law, they would have recognized the voice of God in the warning of His servant; but their minds had become so blinded by rejection of light that they really believed Noah's message to be a delusion.

It was not multitudes or majorities that were on the side of right. The world was arrayed against God's justice and His laws, and Noah was regarded as a fanatic.

The world was arrayed against God's justice and His laws, and Noah was regarded as a fanatic.

Satan, when tempting Eve to disobey God, said to her, "Ye shall not surely die." Genesis 3:4. Great men, worldly, honored, and wise men, repeated the same. "The threatenings of God," they said, "are for the purpose of intimidating, and will never be verified. You need not be alarmed. Such an event as the destruction of the world by the God who made it, and the punishment of the beings He has created, will never take place. Be at peace; fear not. Noah is a wild fanatic."

The world made merry at the folly of the deluded old man. Instead of humbling the heart before God, they continued their disobedience and wickedness, the same as though God had not spoken to them through His servant.

But Noah stood like a rock amid the tempest. Surrounded by popular contempt and ridicule, he distinguished himself by his holy integrity and unwavering faithfulness. A power attended his words, for it was the voice of God to man through His servant. Connection with God made him strong in the strength of infinite power, while for one hundred and twenty years his solemn voice fell upon the ears of that generation in regard to events, which, so far as human wisdom could judge, were impossible.

Human Reasoning

The world before the Flood reasoned that for centuries the laws of nature had been fixed. The recurring seasons had come in their order. Heretofore rain had never fallen; the earth had been watered by a mist or dew. The rivers had never yet passed their boundaries, but had borne their waters safely to the sea. Fixed decrees had kept the waters from overflowing their banks. But these reasoners did not recognize the hand of Him who had stayed the waters, saying, "Hitherto shalt thou come, but no further." Job 38:11.

As time passed on, with no apparent change in nature, men whose hearts had at times trembled with fear, began to be reassured. They reasoned, as many reason now, that nature is above the God of nature, and that her laws are so firmly established that God Himself could not change them.

They reasoned, as many reason now, that nature is above the God of nature.

Reasoning that if the message of Noah were correct, nature would be turned out of her course, they made that message, in the minds of the world, a delusion—a grand deception. They manifested their contempt for the warning of God by doing just as they had done before the warning was given.

They continued their festivities and their gluttonous feasts; they ate and drank, planted and builded, laying their plans in reference to advantages they hoped to gain in the future; and they went to greater lengths in wickedness, and in defiant disregard of God's requirements, to testify that they had no fear of the Infinite One. They asserted that if there were any truth in what Noah had said, the men of renown—the wise, the prudent, the great men—would understand the matter. Had the antediluvians believed the warning, and repented of their evil deeds, the Lord would have turned aside His wrath, as he afterward did from Nineveh. But by their obstinate resistance to the reproofs of conscience and the warnings of God's prophet, that generation filled up the measure of their iniquity, and became ripe for destruction.

Noah's Last Appeal

The period of their probation was about to expire. Noah had faithfully followed the instructions which he had received from God. The ark was finished in every part as the Lord had directed, and was stored with food for man and beast. And now the servant of God made his last solemn appeal to the people. With an agony of desire that words cannot express, he entreated them to seek a refuge while it might be found.

Had the antediluvians believed the warning, and repented of their evil deeds, the Lord would have turned aside His wrath.

Again they rejected his words, and raised their voices in jest and scoffing. Suddenly a silence fell upon the mocking throng. Beasts of every description, the fiercest as well as the most gentle, were seen coming from mountain and forest and quietly making their way toward the ark. A noise as of a rushing wind was heard, and lo, birds were flocking from all directions, their numbers darkening the heavens, and in perfect order they passed to the ark. Animals obeyed the command of God, while men were disobedient. Guided by holy angels, they "went in two and two unto Noah into the ark," and the clean beasts by sevens.

The world looked on in wonder, some in fear. Philosophers were called upon to account for the singular occurrence, but in vain. It was a mystery which they could not fathom. But men had become so hardened by their persistent rejection of light that even this scene produced but a momentary impression.

As the doomed race beheld the sun shining in its glory, and the earth clad in almost Eden beauty, they banished their rising fears by boisterous merriment, and by their deeds of violence they seemed to invite upon themselves the visitation of the already awakened wrath of God.

Chapter 2

Based on Genesis 6 and 7.

Destruction By Water

The Flood—Part II

God commanded Noah, "Come thou and all thy house into the ark; for thee have I seen righteous before Me in this generation." Noah's warnings had been rejected by the world, but his influence and example resulted in blessings to his family. As a reward for his faithfulness and integrity, God saved all the members of his family with him. What encouragement to parental fidelity!

Mercy had ceased its pleadings for the guilty race. The beasts of the field and the birds of the air had entered the place of refuge. Noah and his household were within the ark, "and the Lord shut him in."

A flash of dazzling light was seen, and a cloud of glory more vivid than the lightning descended from heaven and hovered before the entrance of the ark. The massive door, which it was impossible for those within to close, was slowly swung to its place by unseen hands.

Noah was shut in, and the rejecters of God's mercy were shut out. The seal of Heaven was on that door; God had shut it, and God alone could open it. So when Christ shall cease His intercession for guilty men, before His coming in the clouds of heaven, the door of mercy will be shut. Then divine grace will no longer restrain the wicked, and Satan will have full control of those who have rejected mercy. They will endeavor to destroy God's people; but as Noah was shut into the ark, so the righteous will be shielded by divine power.

Noah was shut in, and the rejecters of God's mercy were shut out.

For seven days after Noah and his family entered the ark, there appeared no sign of the coming storm. During this period their faith was tested. It was a time of triumph to the world without. The apparent delay confirmed them in the belief that Noah's message was a delusion, and that the Flood would never come.

Notwithstanding the solemn scenes which they had witnessed—the beasts and birds entering the ark, and the angel of God closing the door—they still continued their sport and revelry, even making a jest of these signal manifestations of God's power. They gathered in crowds about the ark, deriding its inmates with a daring violence which they had never ventured upon before.

The Destruction

But upon the eighth day dark clouds overspread the heavens. There followed the muttering of thunder and the flash of lightning. Soon large drops of rain began to fall. The world had never witnessed anything like this, and the hearts of men were struck with fear. All were secretly inquiring, "Can it be that Noah was in the right, and that the world is doomed to destruction?"

Darker and darker grew the heavens, and faster came the falling rain. The beasts were roaming about in the wildest terror, and their discordant cries seemed to moan out their own destiny and the fate of man.

Then "the fountains of the great deep" were "broken up, and the windows of heaven were opened." Water appeared to come from the clouds in mighty cataracts. Rivers broke away from their boundaries, and overflowed the valleys. Jets of water burst from the earth with indescribable force, throwing massive rocks hundreds of feet into the air, and these, in falling, buried themselves deep in the ground.

The terror of man and beast was beyond description.

The people first beheld the destruction of the works of their own hands. Their splendid buildings, and the beautiful gardens and groves where they had placed their idols, were destroyed by lightning from heaven, and the ruins were scattered far and wide. The altars on which human sacrifices had been offered were torn down, and the worshipers were made to tremble at the power of the living God, and to know that it was their corruption and idolatry which had called down their destruction.

As the violence of the storm increased, trees, buildings, rocks, and earth were hurled in every direction. The terror of man and beast was beyond description. Above the roar of the tempest was heard the wailing of a people that had despised the authority of God.

Satan himself, who was compelled to remain in the midst of the warring elements, feared for his own existence. He had delighted to control so powerful a race, and desired them to live to practice their abominations and continue their rebellion against the Ruler of heaven. He now uttered imprecations against God, charging Him with injustice and cruelty.

Many of the people, like Satan, blasphemed God, and had they been able, they would have torn Him from the throne of power.

Others were frantic with fear, stretching their hands toward the ark and pleading for admittance. But their entreaties were in vain. Conscience was at last aroused to know that there is a God who ruleth in the heavens. They called upon Him earnestly, but His ear was not open to their cry. In that terrible hour they saw that the transgression of God's law had caused their ruin.

In that terrible hour they saw that the transgression of God's law had caused their ruin.

Yet while, through fear of punishment, they acknowledged their sin, they felt no true contrition, no abhorrence of evil. They would have returned to their defiance of Heaven, had the judgment been removed. So when God's judgments shall fall upon the earth before its deluge by fire, the impenitent will know just where and what their sin is—the despising of His holy law. Yet they will have no more true repentance than did the old-world sinners.

Some in their desperation endeavored to break into the ark, but the firm-made structure withstood their efforts. Some clung to the ark until they were borne away by the surging waters, or their hold was broken by collision with rocks and trees. The massive ark trembled in every fiber as it was beaten by the merciless winds and flung from billow to billow. The cries of the beasts within expressed their fear and pain. But amid the warring elements it continued to ride safely. Angels that excel in strength were commissioned to preserve it.

Angels that excel in strength were commissioned to preserve it.

The beasts, exposed to the tempest, rushed toward man, as though expecting help from him. Some of the people bound their children and themselves upon powerful animals, knowing that these were tenacious of life, and would climb to the highest points to escape the rising waters.

Some fastened themselves to lofty trees on the summit of hills or mountains; but the trees were uprooted, and with their burden of living beings were hurled into the seething billows. One spot after another that promised safety was abandoned.

As the waters rose higher and higher, the people fled for refuge to the loftiest mountains. Often man and beast would struggle together for a foothold, until both were swept away.

From the highest peaks men looked abroad upon a shoreless ocean. The solemn warnings of God's servant no longer seemed a subject for ridicule and scorning. How those doomed sinners longed for the opportunities which they had slighted! How they pleaded for one hour's probation, one more privilege of mercy, one call from the lips of Noah!

But the sweet voice of mercy was no more to be heard by them. Love, no less than justice, demanded that God's judgments should put a check on sin. The avenging waters swept over the last retreat, and the despisers of God perished in the black depths.

Another Storm Is Coming

"By the word of God … the world that then was, being overflowed with water, perished: but the heavens and the earth, which are now, by the same word are kept in store, reserved unto fire against the day of judgment and perdition of ungodly men." 2 Peter 3:5–7.

Another storm is coming. The earth will again be swept by the desolating wrath of God, and sin and sinners will be destroyed.

The sins that called for vengeance upon the antediluvian world exist today. The fear of God is banished from the hearts of men, and His law is treated with indifference and contempt. The intense worldliness of that generation is equaled by that of the generation now living.

Said Christ, "As in the days that were before the Flood they were eating and drinking, marrying and giving in marriage, until the day that Noah entered into the ark, and knew not until the Flood came, and took them all away; so shall also the coming of the Son of man be." Matthew 24:38, 39.

The earth will again be swept by the desolating wrath of God, and sin and sinners will be destroyed.

God did not condemn the antediluvians for eating and drinking; He had given them the fruits of the earth in great abundance to supply their physical wants. Their sin consisted in taking these gifts without gratitude to the Giver, and debasing themselves by indulging appetite without restraint.

It was lawful for them to marry. Marriage was in God's order; it was one of the first institutions which He established. He gave special directions concerning this ordinance, clothing it with sanctity and beauty; but these directions were forgotten, and marriage was perverted and made to minister to passion.

Noah's Day and Our Day

A similar condition of things exists now. That which is lawful in itself is carried to excess. Appetite is indulged without restraint. Professed followers of Christ are today eating and drinking with the drunken, while their names stand in honored church records. Intemperance benumbs the moral and spiritual powers and prepares the way for indulgence of the lower passions.

Multitudes feel under no moral obligation to curb their sensual desires, and they become the slaves of lust. Men are living for the pleasures of sense; for this world and this life alone.

Extravagance pervades all circles of society. Integrity is sacrificed for luxury and display.

They that make haste to be rich pervert justice and oppress the poor, and "slaves and souls of men" are still bought and sold. Fraud and bribery and theft stalk unrebuked in high places and in low. The issues of the press teem with records of murder—crimes so cold-blooded and causeless that it seems as though every instinct of humanity were blotted out. And these atrocities have become of so common occurrence that they hardly elicit a comment or awaken surprise.

The spirit of anarchy is permeating all nations, and the outbreaks that from time to time excite the horror of the world are but indications of the pent-up fires of passion and lawlessness that, having once escaped control, will fill the earth with woe and desolation.

These atrocities have become of so common occurrence that they hardly elicit a comment or awaken surprise.

The picture which Inspiration has given of the antediluvian world represents too truly the condition to which modern society is fast hastening. Even now, in the present century, and in professedly Christian lands, there are crimes daily perpetrated as black and terrible as those for which the old-world sinners were destroyed.

Before the Flood God sent Noah to warn the world, that the people might be led to repentance, and thus escape the threatened destruction. As the time of Christ's second appearing draws near, the Lord sends His servants with a warning to the world to prepare for that great event.

Multitudes have been living in transgression of God's law, and now He in mercy calls them to obey its sacred precepts. All who will put away their sins by repentance toward God and faith in Christ are offered pardon. But many feel that it requires too great a sacrifice to put away sin. Because their life does not harmonize with the pure principles of God's moral government, they reject His warnings and deny the authority of His law.

Of the vast population of the earth before the Flood, only eight souls believed and obeyed God's word through Noah. For a hundred and twenty years the preacher of righteousness warned the world of the coming destruction, but his message was rejected and despised. So it will be now.

Before the Lawgiver shall come to punish the disobedient, transgressors are warned to repent, and return to their allegiance.

Before the Lawgiver shall come to punish the disobedient, transgressors are warned to repent, and return to their allegiance; but with the majority these warnings will be in vain.

False Doctrine of Millenium

Says the apostle Peter, "There shall come in the last days scoffers, walking after their own lusts, and saying, Where is the promise of His coming? for since the fathers fell asleep, all things continue as they were from the beginning." 2 Peter 3:3, 4.

Do we not hear these very words repeated, not merely by the openly ungodly, but by many who occupy the pulpits of our land? "There is no cause for alarm," they cry. "Before Christ shall come, all the world is to be converted, and righteousness is to reign for a thousand years. Peace, peace! all things continue as they were from the beginning. Let none be disturbed by the exciting message of these alarmists."

But this doctrine of the millennium does not harmonize with the teachings of Christ and His apostles. Jesus asked the significant question, "When the Son of man cometh, shall He find faith on the earth?" Luke 18:8. And, as we have seen, He declares that the state of the world will be as in the days of Noah.

Paul warns us that we may look for wickedness to increase as the end draws near: "The Spirit speaketh expressly, that in the latter times some shall depart from the faith, giving heed to seducing spirits, and doctrines of devils." 1 Timothy 4:1. The apostle says that "in the last days perilous times shall come." 2 Timothy 3:1. And he gives a startling list of sins that will be found among those who have a form of godliness.

Amusement and Pleasure Seeking

As the time of their probation was closing, the antediluvians gave themselves up to exciting amusements and festivities. Those who possessed influence and power were bent on keeping the minds of the people engrossed with mirth and pleasure, lest any should be impressed by the last solemn warning. Do we not see the same repeated in our day?

While God's servants are giving the message that the end of all things is at hand, the world is absorbed in amusements and pleasure seeking. There is a constant round of excitement that causes indifference to God and prevents the people from being impressed by the truths which alone can save them from the coming destruction.

Reasoning of Philosophy

In Noah's day philosophers declared that it was impossible for the world to be destroyed by water; so now there are men of science who endeavor to show that the world cannot be destroyed by fire—that this would be inconsistent with the laws of nature. But the God of nature, the Maker and Controller of her laws, can use the works of His hands to serve His own purpose.

In Noah's day philosophers declared that it was impossible for the world to be destroyed by water.

When great and wise men had proved to their satisfaction that it was impossible for the world to be destroyed by water, when the fears of the people were quieted, when all regarded Noah's prophecy as a delusion, and looked upon him as a fanatic—then it was that God's time had come.

"The fountains of the great deep" were "broken up, and the windows of heaven were opened," and the scoffers were overwhelmed in the waters of the Flood. With all their boasted philosophy, men found too late that their wisdom was foolishness, that the Lawgiver is greater than the laws of nature, and that Omnipotence is at no loss for means to accomplish His purposes.

"As it was in the days of Noah," "even thus shall it be in the days when the Son of man is revealed." Luke 17:26, 30. "The day of the Lord will come as a thief in the night; in the which the heavens shall pass away with a great noise, and the elements shall melt with fervent heat, the earth also and the works that are therein shall be burned up." 2 Peter 3:10.

When the reasoning of philosophy has banished the fear of God's judgments; when religious teachers are pointing forward to long ages of peace and prosperity, and the world are absorbed in their rounds of business and pleasure, planting and building, feasting and merrymaking, rejecting God's warnings and mocking His messengers—then it is that sudden destruction cometh upon them, and they shall not escape. 1 Thessalonians 5:3.

Chapter 3

Based on Genesis 7:20–9:17.

The Rainbow Sign

After the Flood

The waters rose fifteen cubits above the highest mountains. It often seemed to the family within the ark that they must perish, as for five long months their boat was tossed about, apparently at the mercy of wind and wave. It was a trying ordeal; but Noah's faith did not waver, for he had the assurance that the divine hand was upon the helm.

As the waters began to subside, the Lord caused the ark to drift into a spot protected by a group of mountains that had been preserved by His power. These mountains were but a little distance apart, and the ark moved about in this quiet haven, and was no longer driven upon the boundless ocean. This gave great relief to the weary, tempest-tossed voyagers.

Noah and his family anxiously waited for the decrease of the waters, for they longed to go forth again upon the earth. Forty days after the tops of the mountains became visible, they sent out a raven, a bird of quick scent, to discover whether the earth had become dry. This bird, finding nothing but water, continued to fly to and from the ark.

Seven days later a dove was sent forth, which, finding no footing, returned to the ark. Noah waited seven days longer, and again sent forth the dove. When she returned at evening with an olive leaf in her mouth, there was great rejoicing.

Later "Noah removed the covering of the ark, and looked, and, behold, the face of the ground was dry." Still he waited patiently within the ark. As he had entered at God's command, he waited for special directions to depart.

At last an angel descended from heaven, opened the massive door, and bade the patriarch and his household go forth upon the earth and take with them every living thing.

In the joy of their release Noah did not forget Him by whose gracious care they had been preserved. His first act after leaving the ark was to build an altar and offer from every kind of clean beast and fowl a sacrifice, thus manifesting his gratitude to God for deliverance and his faith in Christ, the great sacrifice.

As he had entered at God's command, he waited for special directions to depart.

This offering was pleasing to the Lord; and a blessing resulted, not only to the patriarch and his family, but to all who should live upon the earth. "The Lord smelled a sweet savor; and the Lord said in His heart, I will not again curse the ground any more for man's sake. … While the earth remaineth, seedtime and harvest, and cold and heat, and summer and winter, and day and night shall not cease."

Here was a lesson for all succeeding generations. Noah had come forth upon a desolate earth, but before preparing a house for himself he built an altar to God. His stock of cattle was small, and had been preserved at great expense; yet he cheerfully gave a part to the Lord as an acknowledgment that all was His.

In like manner it should be our first care to render our freewill offerings to God. Every manifestation of His mercy and love toward us should be gratefully acknowledged, both by acts of devotion and by gifts to His cause.

The Rainbow Promise

Lest the gathering clouds and falling rain should fill men with constant terror, from fear of another flood, the Lord encouraged the family of Noah by a promise: "I will establish My covenant with you; … neither shall there any more be a flood to destroy the earth. … I do set My bow in the cloud, and it shall be for a token of a covenant between Me and the earth. And it shall come to pass, when I bring a cloud over the earth, that the bow shall be seen in the cloud. … And I will look upon it, that I may remember the everlasting covenant between God and every living creature."

How great the condescension of God and His compassion for His erring creatures in thus placing the beautiful rainbow in the clouds as a token of His covenant with men!

The Lord declares that when He looks upon the bow, He will remember His covenant. This does not imply that He would ever forget; but He speaks to us in our own language, that we may better understand Him.

The Most High had bended the bow and placed it in the clouds as an assurance that the waters should never again overflow the earth.

It was God's purpose that as the children of after generations should ask the meaning of the glorious arch which spans the heavens, their parents should repeat the story of the Flood, and tell them that the Most High had bended the bow and placed it in the clouds as an assurance that the waters should never again overflow the earth. Thus from generation to generation it would testify of divine love to man and would strengthen his confidence in God.

In heaven the semblance of a rainbow encircles the throne and overarches the head of Christ. The prophet says, "As the appearance of the bow that is in the cloud in the day of rain, so was the appearance of the brightness round about [the throne]. This was the appearance of the likeness of the glory of Jehovah." Ezekiel 1:28.

The revelator declares, "Behold, a throne was set in heaven, and one sat on the throne. … There was a rainbow round about the throne, in sight like unto an emerald." Revelation 4:2, 3.

When man by his great wickedness invites the divine judgments, the Saviour, interceding with the Father in his behalf, points to the bow in the clouds, to the rainbow around the throne and above His own head, as a token of the mercy of God toward the repentant sinner.

With the assurance given to Noah concerning the Flood, God Himself has linked one of the most precious promises of His grace: "As I have sworn that the waters of Noah should no more go over the earth; so have I sworn that I would not be wroth with thee, nor rebuke thee. For the mountains shall depart, and the hills be removed; but My kindness shall not depart from thee, neither shall the covenant of My peace be removed, saith Jehovah that hath mercy on thee." Isaiah 54:9, 10.

As Noah looked upon the powerful beasts of prey that came forth with him from the ark, he feared that his family, numbering only eight persons, would be destroyed by them. But the Lord sent an angel to His servant with the assuring message: "The fear of you and the dread of you shall be upon every beast of the earth, and upon every fowl of the air, upon all that moveth upon the earth, and upon all the fishes of the sea; into your hand are they delivered. Every moving thing that liveth shall be meat for you; even as the green herb have I given you all things."

Before this time God had given man no permission to eat animal food; He intended that the race should subsist wholly upon the productions of the earth; but now that every green thing had been destroyed, He allowed them to eat the flesh of the clean beasts that had been preserved in the ark.

Changes on the Earth's Surface

The entire surface of the earth was changed at the Flood. A third dreadful curse rested upon it in consequence of sin. As the water began to subside, the hills and mountains were surrounded by a vast, turbid sea, Everywhere were strewn the dead bodies of men and beasts. The Lord would not permit these to remain to decompose and pollute the air, therefore He made of the earth a vast burial ground.

A violent wind which was caused to blow for the purpose of drying up the waters, moved them with great force, in some instances even carrying away the tops of the mountains and heaping up trees, rocks, and earth above the bodies of the dead.

By the same means the silver and gold, the choice wood and precious stones, which had enriched and adorned the world before the Flood, and which the inhabitants had idolized, were concealed from the sight and search of men, the violent action of the waters piling earth and rocks upon these treasures, and in some cases even forming mountains above them. God saw that the more He enriched and prospered sinful men, the more they would corrupt their ways before Him. The treasures that should have led them to glorify the bountiful Giver had been worshiped, while God had been dishonored and despised.

The earth presented an appearance of confusion and desolation impossible to describe. The mountains, once so beautiful in their perfect symmetry, had become broken and irregular. Stones, ledges, and ragged rocks were now scattered upon the surface of the earth.

In many places hills and mountains had disappeared, leaving no trace where they once stood; and plains had given place to mountain ranges. These changes were more marked in some places than in others.

Where once had been earth's richest treasures of gold, silver, and precious stones, were seen the heaviest marks of the curse. And upon countries that were not inhabited, and those where there had been the least crime, the curse rested more lightly.

At this time immense forests were buried. These have since been changed to coal, forming the extensive coal beds that now exist, and also yielding large quantities of oil. The coal and oil frequently ignite and burn beneath the surface of the earth. Thus rocks are heated, limestone is burned, and iron ore melted. The action of the water upon the lime adds fury to the intense heat, and causes earthquakes, volcanoes, and fiery issues.

As the fire and water come in contact with ledges of rock and ore, there are heavy explosions underground, which sound like muffled thunder. The air is hot and suffocating. Volcanic eruptions follow; and these often failing to give sufficient vent to the heated elements, the earth itself is convulsed, the ground heaves and swells like the waves of the sea, great fissures appear, and sometimes cities, villages, and burning mountains are swallowed up.

These wonderful manifestations will be more and more frequent and terrible just before the second coming of Christ and the end of the world, as signs of its speedy destruction.

The Coming Judgment

The depths of the earth are the Lord's arsenal, whence were drawn weapons to be employed in the destruction of the old world. Waters gushing from the earth united with the waters from heaven to accomplish the work of desolation.

Since the Flood, fire as well as water has been God's agent to destroy very wicked cities.

Since the Flood, fire as well as water has been God's agent to destroy very wicked cities. These judgments are sent that those who lightly regard God's law and trample upon His authority may be led to tremble before His power and to confess His just sovereignty.

As men have beheld burning mountains pouring forth fire and flames and torrents of melted ore, drying up rivers, overwhelming populous cities, and everywhere spreading ruin and desolation, the stoutest heart has been filled with terror and infidels and blasphemers have been constrained to acknowledge the infinite power of God.

Said the prophets of old, referring to scenes like these: "Oh that Thou wouldest rend the heavens, that Thou wouldest come down, that the mountains might flow down at Thy presence, as when the melting fire burneth, the fire causeth the waters to boil, to make Thy name known to Thine adversaries, that the nations may tremble at Thy presence! When Thou didst terrible things which we looked not for, Thou camest down, the mountains flowed down at Thy presence." Isaiah 64:1–3.

"The Lord hath His way in the whirlwind and in the storm, and the clouds are the dust of His feet. He rebuketh the sea, and maketh it dry, and drieth up all the rivers." Nahum 1:3, 4.

More terrible manifestations than the world has ever yet beheld, will be witnessed at the second advent of Christ. "The mountains quake at Him, and the hills melt, and the earth is burned at His presence, yea, the world, and all that dwell therein. Who can stand before His indignation? and who can abide in the fierceness of His anger?" Nahum 1:5, 6.

"Bow Thy heavens, O Lord, and come down: touch the mountains, and they shall smoke. Cast forth lightning, and scatter them: shoot out Thine arrows, and destroy them." Psalm 144:5, 6.

More terrible manifestations than the world has ever yet beheld, will be witnessed at the second advent of Christ.

"I will show wonders in heaven above, and signs in the earth beneath; blood, and fire, and vapor of smoke." Acts 2:19. "And there were voices, and thunders, and lightnings; and there was a great earthquake, such as was not since men were upon the earth, so mighty an earthquake, and so great." "And every island fled away, and the mountains were not found. And there fell upon men a great hail out of heaven, every stone about the weight of a talent." Revelation 16:18, 20, 21.

As lightnings from heaven unite with the fire in the earth, the mountains will burn like a furnace, and will pour forth terrific streams of lava, overwhelming gardens and fields, villages and cities. Seething molten masses thrown into the rivers will cause the waters to boil, sending forth massive rocks with indescribable violence and scattering their broken fragments upon the land. Rivers will be dried up. The earth will be convulsed; everywhere there will be dreadful earthquakes and eruptions.

Thus God will destroy the wicked from off the earth. But the righteous will be preserved in the midst of these commotions, as Noah was preserved in the ark. God will be their refuge, and under His wings shall they trust. Says the psalmist: "Because thou hast made the Lord, which is my refuge, even the Most High, thy habitation; there shall no evil befall thee." Psalm 91:9, 10.

"In the time of trouble He shall hide me in His pavilion: in the secret of His tabernacle shall He hide me." Psalm 27:5. God's promise is, "Because he hath set his love upon Me, therefore will I deliver him: I will set him on high, because he hath known My name." Psalm 91:14.

Chapter 4

Based on Genesis 1 and 2; Exodus 20:8–11.

Skepticism Over Creation and the Flood

The Literal Week

Like the Sabbath, the week originated at creation, and it has been preserved and brought down to us through Bible history. God Himself measured off the first week as a sample for successive weeks to the close of time. Like every other, it consisted of seven literal days. Six days were employed in the work of creation; upon the seventh, God rested, and He then blessed this day and set it apart as a day of rest for man.

In the law given from Sinai, God recognized the week, and the facts upon which it is based. After giving the command, "Remember the Sabbath day, to keep it holy," and specifying what shall be done on the six days, and what shall not be done on the seventh, He states the reason for thus observing the week, by pointing back to His own example: "For in six days the Lord made heaven and earth, the sea, and all that in them is, and rested the seventh day: wherefore the Lord blessed the Sabbath day, and hallowed it." Exodus 20:8–11.

The Weekly Sabbath vs. Long Ages of Creation

This reason appears beautiful and forcible when we understand the days of creation to be literal. The first six days of each week are given to man for labor, because God employed the same period of the first week in the work of creation. On the seventh day man is to refrain from labor, in commemoration of the Creator's rest.

On the seventh day man is to refrain from labor, in commemoration of the Creator's rest.

But the assumption that the events of the first week required thousands upon thousands of years, strikes directly at the foundation of the fourth commandment. It represents the Creator as commanding men to observe the week of literal days in commemoration of vast, indefinite periods. This is unlike His method of dealing with His creatures. It makes indefinite and obscure that which He has made very plain. It is infidelity in its most insidious and hence most dangerous form; its real character is so disguised that it is held and taught by many who profess to believe the Bible.

"By the word of the Lord were the heavens made; and all the host of them by the breath of His mouth." "For He spake, and it was done; He commanded, and it stood fast." Psalm 33:6, 9.

The Bible recognizes no long ages in which the earth was slowly evolved from chaos. Of each successive day of creation, the sacred record declares that it consisted of the evening and the morning, like all other days that have followed. At the close of each day is given the result of the Creator's work. The statement is made at the close of the first week's record, "These are the generations of the heavens and of the earth when they were created." Genesis 2:4.

But this does not convey the idea that the days of creation were other than literal days. Each day was called a generation, because that in it God generated, or produced, some new portion of His work.

The Flood and Geology

Geologists claim to find evidence from the earth itself that it is very much older than the Mosaic record teaches. Bones of men and animals, as well as instruments of warfare, petrified trees, et cetera, much larger than any that now exist, or that have existed for thousands of years, have been discovered, and from this it is inferred that the earth was populated long before the time brought to view in the record of creation, and by a race of beings vastly superior in size to any men now living. Such reasoning has led many professed Bible believers to adopt the position that the days of creation were vast, indefinite periods.

But apart from Bible history, geology can prove nothing. Those who reason so confidently upon its discoveries have no adequate conception of the size of men, animals, and trees before the Flood, or of the great changes which then took place. Relics found in the earth do give evidence of conditions differing in many respects from the present, but the time when these conditions existed can be learned only from the Inspired Record.

In the history of the Flood, inspiration has explained that which geology alone could never fathom.

In the history of the Flood, inspiration has explained that which geology alone could never fathom.

In the days of Noah, men, animals, and trees, many times larger than now exist, were buried, and thus preserved as an evidence to later generations that the antediluvians perished by a flood. God designed that the discovery of these things should establish faith in inspired history; but men, with their vain reasoning, fall into the same error as did the people before the Flood—the things which God gave them as a benefit, they turn into a curse by making a wrong use of them.

It is one of Satan's devices to lead the people to accept the fables of infidelity; for he can thus obscure the law of God, in itself very plain, and embolden men to rebel against the divine government. His efforts are especially directed against the fourth commandment, because it so clearly points to the living God, the Maker of the heavens and the earth.

Science and The Word of God

There is a constant effort made to explain the work of creation as the result of natural causes; and human reasoning is accepted even by professed Christians, in opposition to plain Scripture facts. There are many who oppose the investigation of the prophecies, especially those of Daniel and the Revelation, declaring them to be so obscure that we cannot understand them; yet these very persons eagerly receive the suppositions of geologists, in contradiction of the Mosaic record.

But if that which God has revealed is so difficult to understand, how inconsistent it is to accept mere suppositions in regard to that which He has not revealed!

Human science cannot search out the secrets of the Most High.

"The secret things belong unto the Lord our God: but those things which are revealed belong unto us and to our children forever." Deuteronomy 29:29. Just how God accomplished the work of creation He has never revealed to men; human science cannot search out the secrets of the Most High. His creative power is as incomprehensible as His existence.

God has permitted a flood of light to be poured upon the world in both science and art; but when professedly scientific men treat upon these subjects from a merely human point of view, they will assuredly come to wrong conclusions.

It may be innocent to speculate beyond what God's word has revealed, if our theories do not contradict facts found in the Scriptures; but those who leave the word of God, and seek to account for His created works upon scientific principles, are drifting without chart or compass upon an unknown ocean.

The greatest minds, if not guided by the word of God in their research, become bewildered in their attempts to trace the relations of science and revelation. Because the Creator and His works are so far beyond their comprehension that they are unable to explain them by natural laws, they regard Bible history as unreliable.

Those who doubt the reliability of the records of the Old and New Testaments, will be led to go a step further, and doubt the existence of God; and then, having lost their anchor, they are left to beat about upon the rocks of infidelity.

These persons have lost the simplicity of faith. There should be a settled belief in the divine authority of God's Holy Word. The Bible is not to be tested by men's ideas of science. Human knowledge is an unreliable guide. Skeptics who read the Bible for the sake of caviling, may, through an imperfect comprehension of either science or revelation, claim to find contradictions between them; but rightly understood, they are in perfect harmony.

Those who doubt the reliability of the records of the Old and New Testaments, will be led to go a step further.

Moses wrote under the guidance of the Spirit of God, and a correct theory of geology will never claim discoveries that cannot be reconciled with his statements. All truth, whether in nature or in revelation, is consistent with itself in all its manifestations.

In the word of God many queries are raised that the most profound scholars can never answer. Attention is called to these subjects to show us how much there is, even among the common things of everyday life, that finite minds, with all their boasted wisdom, can never fully understand.

Yet men of science think that they can comprehend the wisdom of God, that which He has done or can do. The idea largely prevails that He is restricted by His own laws. Men either deny or ignore His existence, or think to explain everything, even the operation of His Spirit upon the human heart; and they no longer reverence His name or fear His power. They do not believe in the supernatural, not understanding God's laws or His infinite power to work His will through them.

As commonly used, the term "laws of nature" comprises what men have been able to discover with regard to the laws that govern the physical world; but how limited is their knowledge, and how vast the field in which the Creator can work in harmony with His own laws and yet wholly beyond the comprehension of finite beings!

God and the Laws of Nature

Many teach that matter possesses vital power—that certain properties are imparted to matter, and it is then left to act through its own inherent energy; and that the operations of nature are conducted in harmony with fixed laws, with which God Himself cannot interfere. This is false science, and is not sustained by the word of God.

Nature is the servant of her Creator.

Nature is the servant of her Creator. God does not annul His laws or work contrary to them, but He is continually using them as His instruments. Nature testifies of an intelligence, a presence, an active energy, that works in and through her laws. There is in nature the continual working of the Father and the Son. Christ says, "My Father worketh hitherto, and I work." John 5:17.

The Levites, in their hymn recorded by Nehemiah, sang, "Thou, even Thou, art Lord alone; Thou hast made heaven, the heaven of heavens, with all their host, the earth, and all things therein, … and Thou *preservest* them all." Nehemiah 9:6.

As regards this world, God's work of creation is completed. For "the works were finished from the foundation of the world." Hebrews 4:3. But His energy is still exerted in upholding the objects of His creation. It is not because the mechanism that has once been set in motion continues to act by its own inherent energy that the pulse beats and breath follows breath; but every breath, every pulsation of the heart, is an evidence of the all-pervading care of Him in whom "we live, and move, and have our being." Acts 17:28.

It is not because of inherent power that year by year the earth produces her bounties and continues her motion around the sun. The hand of God guides the planets and keeps them in position in their orderly march through the heavens. He "bringeth out their host by number: He calleth them all by names by the greatness of His might, for that He is strong in power; not one faileth." Isaiah 40:26.

It is through His power that vegetation flourishes, that the leaves appear and the flowers bloom. He "maketh grass to grow upon the mountains" (Psalm 147:8), and by Him the valleys are made fruitful. "All the beasts of the forest … seek their meat from God," and every living creature, from the smallest insect up to man, is daily dependent upon His providential care.

In the beautiful words of the psalmist, "These wait all upon Thee. … That Thou givest them they gather: Thou openest Thine hand, they are filled with good." Psalm 104:20, 21, 27, 28. His word controls the elements; He covers the heavens with clouds and prepares rain for the earth. "He giveth snow like wool: He scattereth the hoarfrost like ashes." Psalm 147:16.

"When He uttereth His voice, there is a multitude of waters in the heavens, and He causeth the vapors to ascend from the ends of the earth; He maketh lightnings with rain, and bringeth forth the wind out of His treasuries." Jeremiah 10:13.

God is the foundation of everything. All true science is in harmony with His works; all true education leads to obedience to His government. Science opens new wonders to our view; she soars high, and explores new depths; but she brings nothing from her research that conflicts with divine revelation. Ignorance may seek to support false views of God by appeals to science, but the book of nature and the written word shed light upon each other. We are thus led to adore the Creator and to have an intelligent trust in His word.

All true science is in harmony with His works; all true education leads to obedience to His government.

No finite mind can fully comprehend the existence, the power, the wisdom, or the works of the Infinite One. Says the sacred writer: "Canst thou by searching find out God? canst thou find out the Almighty unto perfection? It is as high as heaven; what canst thou do? deeper than hell; what canst thou know? The measure thereof is longer than the earth, and broader than the sea." Job 11:7–9.

The mightiest intellects of earth cannot comprehend God. Men may be ever searching, ever learning, and still there is an infinity beyond.

Yet the works of creation testify of God's power and greatness. "The heavens declare the glory of God; and the firmament showeth His handiwork." Psalm 19:1. Those who take the written word as their counselor will find in science an aid to understand God. "The invisible things of Him from the creation of the world are clearly seen, being understood by the things that are made, even His eternal power and Godhead." Romans 1:20.

Chapter 5

Based on Genesis 9:25–27; 11:1–9.

Descendants of Noah and the Tower of Babel

The Tower of Babel

To repeople the desolate earth, which the Flood had so lately swept from its moral corruption, God had preserved but one family, the household of Noah, to whom He had declared, "Thee have I seen righteous before Me in this generation." Genesis 7:1. Yet in the three sons of Noah was speedily developed the same great distinction seen in the world before the Flood. In Shem, Ham, and Japheth, who were to be the founders of the human race, was foreshadowed the character of their posterity.

Noah's Descendants

Noah, speaking by divine inspiration, foretold the history of the three great races to spring from these fathers of mankind. Tracing the descendants of Ham, through the son rather than the father, he declared, "Cursed be Canaan; a servant of servants shall he be unto his brethren." The unnatural crime of Ham declared that filial reverence had long before been cast from his soul, and it revealed the impiety and vileness of his character. These evil characteristics were perpetuated in Canaan and his posterity, whose continued guilt called upon them the judgments of God.

On the other hand, the reverence manifested by Shem and Japheth for their father, and thus for the divine statutes, promised a brighter future for their descendants. Concerning these sons it was declared: "Blessed be Jehovah, God of Shem; and Canaan shall be his servant. God shall enlarge Japheth, and he shall dwell in the tents of Shem; and Canaan shall be his servant."

The line of Shem was to be that of the chosen people, of God's covenant, of the promised Redeemer. Jehovah was the God of Shem. From him would descend Abraham, and the people of Israel, through whom Christ was to come. "Happy is that people, whose God is the Lord." Psalm 144:15.

And Japheth "shall dwell in the tents of Shem." In the blessings of the gospel the descendants of Japheth were especially to share.

The posterity of Canaan descended to the most degrading forms of heathenism. Though the prophetic curse had doomed them to slavery, the doom was withheld for centuries. God bore with their impiety and corruption until they passed the limits of divine forbearance. Then they were dispossessed, and became bondmen to the descendants of Shem and Japheth.

The prophecy of Noah was no arbitrary denunciation of wrath or declaration of favor. It did not fix the character and destiny of his sons. But it showed what would be the result of the course of life they had severally chosen and the character they had developed. It was an expression of God's purpose toward them and their posterity in view of their own character and conduct.

As a rule, children inherit the dispositions and tendencies of their parents, and imitate their example; so that the sins of the parents are practiced by the children from generation to generation. Thus the vileness and irreverence of Ham were reproduced in his posterity, bringing a curse upon them for many generations. "One sinner destroyeth much good." Ecclesiastes 9:18.

On the other hand, how richly rewarded was Shem's respect for his father; and what an illustrious line of holy men appears in his posterity! "The Lord knoweth the days of the upright," "and his seed is blessed." Psalm 37:18, 26. "Know therefore that the Lord thy God He is God, the faithful God, which keepeth covenant and mercy with them that love Him and keep His commandments to a thousand generations." Deuteronomy 7:9.

Unbelief and The Tower of Babel

For a time the descendants of Noah continued to dwell among the mountains where the ark had rested. As their numbers increased, apostasy soon led to division. Those who desired to forget their Creator and to cast off the restraint of His law felt a constant annoyance from the teaching and example of their God-fearing associates, and after a time they decided to separate from the worshipers of God. Accordingly they journeyed to the plain of Shinar, on the banks of the river Euphrates. They were attracted by the beauty of the situation and the fertility of the soil, and upon this plain they determined to make their home.

Here they decided to build a city, and in it a tower of such stupendous height as should render it the wonder of the world. These enterprises were designed to prevent the people from scattering abroad in colonies. God had directed men to disperse throughout the earth, to replenish and subdue it; but these Babel builders determined to keep their community united in one body, and to found a monarchy that should eventually embrace the whole earth.

The dwellers on the plain of Shinar disbelieved God's covenant that He would not again bring a flood upon the earth.

Thus their city would become the metropolis of a universal empire; its glory would command the admiration and homage of the world and render the founders illustrious. The magnificent tower, reaching to the heavens, was intended to stand as a monument of the power and wisdom of its builders, perpetuating their fame to the latest generations.

The dwellers on the plain of Shinar disbelieved God's covenant that He would not again bring a flood upon the earth. Many of them denied the existence of God and attributed the Flood to the operation of natural causes. Others believed in a Supreme Being, and that it was He who had destroyed the antediluvian world; and their hearts, like that of Cain, rose up in rebellion against Him.

One object before them in the erection of the tower was to secure their own safety in case of another deluge. By carrying the structure to a much greater height than was reached by the waters of the Flood, they thought to place themselves beyond all possibility of danger.

And as they would be able to ascend to the region of the clouds, they hoped to ascertain the cause of the Flood.

The whole undertaking was designed to exalt still further the pride of its projectors and to turn the minds of future generations away from God and lead them into idolatry.

The Confusion of Languages

When the tower had been partially completed, a portion of it was occupied as a dwelling place for the builders; other apartments, splendidly furnished and adorned, were devoted to their idols. The people rejoiced in their success, and praised the gods of silver and gold, and set themselves against the Ruler of heaven and earth. Suddenly the work that had been advancing so prosperously was checked. Angels were sent to bring to naught the purpose of the builders.

The tower had reached a lofty height, and it was impossible for the workmen at the top to communicate directly with those at the base; therefore men were stationed at different points, each to receive and report to the one next below him the orders for needed material or other directions concerning the work. As messages were thus passing from one to another the language was confounded, so that material was called for which was not needed, and the directions delivered were often the reverse of those that had been given. Confusion and dismay followed.

All work came to a standstill. There could be no further harmony or co-operation. The builders were wholly unable to account for the strange misunderstandings among them, and in their rage and disappointment they reproached one another. Their confederacy ended in strife and bloodshed. Lightnings from heaven, as an evidence of God's displeasure, broke off the upper portion of the tower and cast it to the ground. Men were made to feel that there is a God who ruleth in the heavens.

Up to this time all men had spoken the same language.

Up to this time all men had spoken the same language; now those that could understand one another's speech united in companies;

some went one way, and some another. "The Lord scattered them abroad from thence upon the face of all the earth." This dispersion was the means of peopling the earth, and thus the Lord's purpose was accomplished through the very means that men had employed to prevent its fulfillment.

But at what a loss to those who had set themselves against God! It was His purpose that as men should go forth to found nations in different parts of the earth they should carry with them a knowledge of His will, that the light of truth might shine undimmed to succeeding generations.

Noah, the faithful preacher of righteousness, lived for three hundred and fifty years after the Flood, Shem for five hundred years, and thus their descendants had an opportunity to become acquainted with the requirements of God and the history of His dealings with their fathers. But they were unwilling to listen to these unpalatable truths; they had no desire to retain God in their knowledge; and by the confusion of tongues they were, in a great measure, shut out from intercourse with those who might have given them light.

The Babel builders had indulged the spirit of murmuring against God. Instead of gratefully remembering His mercy to Adam and His gracious covenant with Noah, they had complained of His severity in expelling the first pair from Eden and destroying the world by a flood.

But while they murmured against God as arbitrary and severe, they were accepting the rule of the cruelest of tyrants. Satan was seeking to bring contempt upon the sacrificial offerings that prefigured the death of Christ; and as the minds of the people were darkened by idolatry, he led them to counterfeit these offerings and sacrifice their own children upon the altars of their gods. As men turned away from God, the divine attributes—justice, purity, and love—were supplanted by oppression, violence, and brutality.

The men of Babel had determined to establish a government that should be independent of God.

The men of Babel had determined to establish a government that should be independent of God. There were some among them, however, who feared the Lord, but who had been deceived by the pretensions of the ungodly and drawn into their schemes. For the sake of these faithful ones the Lord delayed His judgments and gave the people time to reveal their true character. As this was developed, the sons of God labored to turn them from their purpose; but the people were fully united in their Heaven-daring undertaking.

Had they gone on unchecked, they would have demoralized the world in its infancy. Their confederacy was founded in rebellion; a kingdom established for self-exaltation, but in which God was to have no rule or honor. Had this confederacy been permitted, a mighty power would have borne sway to banish righteousness—and with it peace, happiness, and security—from the earth. For the divine statutes, which are "holy and just and good" (Romans 7:12), men were endeavoring to substitute laws to suit the purpose of their own selfish and cruel hearts.

Those that feared the Lord cried unto Him to interpose. "And the Lord came down to see the city and the tower, which the children of men builded." In mercy to the world He defeated the purpose of the tower builders and overthrew the memorial of their daring. In mercy He confounded their speech, thus putting a check on their purposes of rebellion. God bears long with the perversity of men, giving them ample opportunity for repentance; but He marks all their devices to resist the authority of His just and holy law.

In mercy to the world He defeated the purpose of the tower builders and overthrew the memorial of their daring.

From time to time the unseen hand that holds the scepter of government is stretched out to restrain iniquity. Unmistakable evidence is given that the Creator of the universe, the One infinite in wisdom and love and truth, is the Supreme Ruler of heaven and earth, and that none can with impunity defy His power.

The schemes of the Babel builders ended in shame and defeat. The monument to their pride became the memorial of their folly. Yet men are continually pursuing the same course—depending upon self, and rejecting God's law. It is the principle that Satan tried to carry out in heaven; the same that governed Cain in presenting his offering.

Tower Builders in Our Time

There are tower builders in our time. Infidels construct their theories from the supposed deductions of sciences, and reject the revealed word of God. They presume to pass sentence upon God's moral government; they despise His law and boast of the sufficiency of human reason. Then, "because sentence against an evil work is not executed speedily, therefore the heart of the sons of men is fully set in them to do evil." Ecclesiastes 8:11.

The monument to their pride became the memorial of their folly.

In the professedly Christian world many turn away from the plain teachings of the Bible and build up a creed from human speculations and pleasing fables, and they point to their tower as a way to climb up to heaven. Men hang with admiration upon the lips of eloquence while it teaches that the transgressor shall not die, that salvation may be secured without obedience to the law of God. If the professed followers of Christ would accept God's standard, it would bring them into unity; but so long as human wisdom is exalted above His Holy Word, there will be divisions and dissension.

The existing confusion of conflicting creeds and sects is fitly represented by the term "Babylon," which prophecy (Revelation 14:8; 18:2) applies to the world-loving churches of the last days.

Many seek to make a heaven for themselves by obtaining riches and power. They "speak wickedly concerning oppression: they speak loftily" (Psalm 73:8), trampling upon human rights and disregarding divine authority. The proud may be for a time in great power, and may see success in all that they undertake; but in the end they will find only disappointment and wretchedness.

The time of God's investigation is at hand. The Most High will come down to see that which the children of men have builded. His sovereign power will be revealed; the works of human pride will be laid low. "The Lord looketh from heaven; He beholdeth all the sons of men. From the place of His habitation He looketh upon all the inhabitants of the earth." "The Lord bringeth the counsel of the heathen to nought: He maketh the devices of the people of none effect. The counsel of the Lord standeth forever, the thoughts of His heart to all generations." Psalm 33:13, 14, 10, 11.

Part 2

Thought Questions

- *What are the parallels between the destruction by water in Noah's day and the destruction by fire in the days of Lot?*
- *What were the root causes of the sins of Sodom?*
- *How did Christ link the conditions in Noah's day, Lot's day, and our day?*
- *Why did Jesus mix descriptions of the destruction of Jerusalem with the great day of His coming? Why does God always give men warning of coming judgments?*
- *Why does Christ reveal the signs of the nearness of His coming, but not the exact time?*
- *In the light of the signs Jesus gave on the Mount of Olives, what significance should we attach to the global conditions in our world today?*

The Coming Storm

"As it was also in the Days of Lot ..."

And as it was in the days of Noah, so it will be also in the days of the Son of Man ... Likewise ***as it was also in the days of Lot****: They ate, they drank, they bought, they sold, they planted, they built; but on the day that Lot went out of Sodom it rained fire and brimstone from heaven and destroyed them all. Even so will it be in the day when the Son of Man is revealed. (Luke 17:26–30 NKJV, emphasis added)*

For if God ... did not spare the ancient world, but saved Noah, one of eight people, a preacher of righteousness, bringing in the flood on the world of the ungodly; and turning the cities of Sodom and Gomorrah into ashes, condemned them to destruction, making them an example to those who afterward would live ungodly; and delivered righteous Lot, who was oppressed by the filthy conduct of the wicked (for that righteous man, dwelling among them, tormented his righteous soul from day to day by seeing and hearing their lawless deeds)—then the Lord knows how to deliver the godly out of temptations and to reserve the unjust under punishment for the day of judgment. (2 Peter 2:4–9 NKJV)

Chapter 6

Based on Genesis 19.

Sodom's Last Night

Destruction of Sodom—Part I

Fairest among the cities of the Jordan Valley was Sodom, set in a plain which was "as the garden of the Lord" in its fertility and beauty. Here the luxuriant vegetation of the tropics flourished. Here was the home of the palm tree, the olive, and the vine; and flowers shed their fragrance throughout the year. Rich harvests clothed the fields, and flocks and herds covered the encircling hills.

Art and commerce contributed to enrich the proud city of the plain. The treasures of the East adorned her palaces, and the caravans of the desert brought their stores of precious things to supply her marts of trade. With little thought or labor, every want of life could be supplied, and the whole year seemed one round of festivity.

The Roots of Sodom's Sin

The profusion reigning everywhere gave birth to luxury and pride. Idleness and riches make the heart hard that has never been oppressed by want or burdened by sorrow. The love of pleasure was fostered by wealth and leisure, and the people gave themselves up to sensual indulgence.

"Behold," says the prophet, "this was the iniquity of thy sister Sodom, pride, fullness of bread, and abundance of idleness was in her and in her daughters, neither did she strengthen the hand of the poor and needy. And they were haughty, and committed abomination before Me: therefore I took them away as I saw good." Ezekiel 16:49, 50.

There is nothing more desired among men than riches and leisure, and yet these gave birth to the sins that brought destruction upon the cities of the plain. Their useless, idle life made them a prey to Satan's temptations, and they defaced the image of God, and became satanic rather than divine. Idleness is the greatest curse that can fall upon man, for vice and crime follow in its train. It enfeebles the mind, perverts the understanding, and debases the soul. Satan lies in ambush, ready to destroy those who are unguarded, whose leisure gives him opportunity to insinuate himself under some attractive disguise. He is never more successful than when he comes to men in their idle hours.

Idleness is the greatest curse that can fall upon man, for vice and crime follow in its train.

In Sodom there was mirth and revelry, feasting and drunkenness. The vilest and most brutal passions were unrestrained. The people openly defied God and His law and delighted in deeds of violence. Though they had before them the example of the antediluvian world, and knew how the wrath of God had been manifested in their destruction, yet they followed the same course of wickedness.

At the time of Lot's removal to Sodom, corruption had not become universal, and God in His mercy permitted rays of light to shine amid the moral darkness. When Abraham rescued the captives from the Elamites, the attention of the people was called to the true faith.

Abraham was not a stranger to the people of Sodom, and his worship of the unseen God had been a matter of ridicule among them; but his victory over greatly superior forces, and his magnanimous disposition of the prisoners and spoil, excited wonder and admiration. While his skill and valor were extolled, none could avoid the conviction that a divine power had made him conqueror. And his noble and unselfish spirit, so foreign to the self-seeking inhabitants of Sodom, was another evidence of the superiority of the religion which he had honored by his courage and fidelity.

Melchizedek, in bestowing the benediction upon Abraham, had acknowledged Jehovah as the source of his strength and the author of the victory: "Blessed be Abram of the most high God, possessor of heaven and earth: and blessed be the most high God, which hath delivered thine enemies into thy hand." Genesis 14:19, 20. God was speaking to that people by His providence, but the last ray of light was rejected as all before had been.

Toward the Last Night of Sodom

And now the last night of Sodom was approaching. Already the clouds of vengeance cast their shadows over the devoted city. But men perceived it not. While angels drew near on their mission of destruction, men were dreaming of prosperity and pleasure. The last day was like every other that had come and gone. Evening fell upon a scene of loveliness and security. A landscape of unrivaled beauty was bathed in the rays of the declining sun. The coolness of eventide had called forth the inhabitants of the city, and the pleasure-seeking throngs were passing to and fro, intent upon the enjoyment of the hour.

In the twilight two strangers drew near to the city gate. They were apparently travelers coming in to tarry for the night. None could discern in those humble wayfarers the mighty heralds of divine judgment, and little dreamed the gay, careless multitude that in their treatment of these heavenly messengers that very night they would reach the climax of the guilt which doomed their proud city.

Politeness and hospitality were habitual with him; they were a part of his religion.

But there was one man who manifested kindly attention toward the strangers and invited them to his home. Lot did not know their true character, but politeness and hospitality were habitual with him; they were a part of his religion—lessons that he had learned from the example of Abraham. Had he not cultivated a spirit of courtesy, he might have been left to perish with the rest of Sodom. Many a household, in closing its doors against a stranger, has shut out God's messenger, who would have brought blessing and hope and peace.

Every act of life, however small, has its bearing for good or for evil. Faithfulness or neglect in what are apparently the smallest duties may open the door for life's richest blessings or its greatest calamities. It is little things that test the character. It is the unpretending acts of daily self-denial, performed with a cheerful, willing heart, that God smiles upon.

It is little things that test the character.

We are not to live for self, but for others. And it is only by self-forgetfulness, by cherishing a loving, helpful spirit, that we can make our life a blessing. The little attentions, the small, simple courtesies, go far to make up the sum of life's happiness, and the neglect of these constitutes no small share of human wretchedness.

Seeing the abuse to which strangers were exposed in Sodom, Lot made it one of his duties to guard them at their entrance, by offering them entertainment at his own house. He was sitting at the gate as the travelers approached, and upon observing them, he rose from his place to meet them, and bowing courteously, said, "Behold now, my lords, turn in, I pray you, into your servant's house, and tarry all night."

They seemed to decline his hospitality, saying, "Nay; but we will abide in the street." Their object in this answer was twofold—to test the sincerity of Lot and also to appear ignorant of the character of the men of Sodom, as if they supposed it safe to remain in the street at night. Their answer made Lot the more determined not to leave them to the mercy of the rabble. He pressed his invitation until they yielded, and accompanied him to his house.

He had hoped to conceal his intention from the idlers at the gate by bringing the strangers to his home by a circuitous route; but their hesitation and delay, and his persistent urging, caused them to be observed, and before they had retired for the night, a lawless crowd gathered about the house. It was an immense company, youth and aged men alike inflamed by the vilest passions. The strangers had been making inquiry in regard to the character of the city, and Lot had warned them not to venture out of his door that night, when the hooting and jeers of the mob were heard, demanding that the men be brought out to them.

Knowing that if provoked to violence they could easily break into his house, Lot went out to try the effect of persuasion upon them. "I pray you, brethren," he said, "do not so wickedly," using the term "brethren" in the sense of neighbors, and hoping to conciliate them and make them ashamed of their vile purposes. But his words were like oil upon the flames.

Their rage became like the roaring of a tempest. They mocked Lot as making himself a judge over them, and threatened to deal worse with him than they had purposed toward his guests. They rushed upon him, and would have torn him in pieces had he not been rescued by the angels of God. The heavenly messengers "put forth their hand, and pulled Lot into the house to them, and shut to the door."

The events that followed, revealed the character of the guests he had entertained. "They smote the men that were at the door of the house with blindness, both small and great: so that they wearied themselves to find the door." Had they not been visited with double blindness, being given up to hardness of heart, the stroke of God upon them would have caused them to fear, and to desist from their evil work.

The inhabitants of Sodom had passed the limits of divine forbearance.

That last night was marked by no greater sins than many others before it; but mercy, so long slighted, had at last ceased its pleading. The inhabitants of Sodom had passed the limits of divine forbearance—"the hidden boundary between God's patience and His wrath." The fires of His vengeance were about to be kindled in the vale of Siddim.

Warning of Destruction

The angels revealed to Lot the object of their mission: "We will destroy this place, because the cry of them is waxen great before the face of the Lord; and the Lord hath sent us to destroy it." The strangers whom Lot had endeavored to protect, now promised to protect him, and to save also all the members of his family who would flee with him from the wicked city.

The mob had wearied themselves out and departed, and Lot went out to warn his children. He repeated the words of the angels, "Up, get you out of this place; for the Lord will destroy this city." But he seemed to them as one that mocked. They laughed at what they called his superstitious fears. His daughters were influenced by their husbands. They were well enough off where they were. They could see no evidence of danger. Everything was just as it had been. They had great possessions, and they could not believe it possible that beautiful Sodom would be destroyed.

He did not realize the terrible necessity for God's judgments to put a check on sin.

Lot returned sorrowfully to his home and told the story of his failure. Then the angels bade him arise and take his wife and the two daughters who were yet in his house and leave the city. But Lot delayed. Though daily distressed at beholding deeds of violence, he had no true conception of the debasing and abominable iniquity practiced in that vile city. He did not realize the terrible necessity for God's judgments to put a check on sin.

Some of his children clung to Sodom, and his wife refused to depart without them. The thought of leaving those whom he held dearest on earth seemed more than he could bear. It was hard to forsake his luxurious home and all the wealth acquired by the labors of his whole life, to go forth a destitute wanderer. Stupefied with sorrow, he lingered, loath to depart. But for the angels of God, they would all have perished in the ruin of Sodom. The heavenly messengers took him and his wife and daughters by the hand and led them out of the city.

Here the angels left them, and turned back to Sodom to accomplish their work of destruction. Another—He with whom Abraham had pleaded—drew near to Lot. In all the cities of the plain, even ten righteous persons had not been found; but in answer to the patriarch's prayer, the one man who feared God was snatched from destruction.

The command was given with startling vehemence: "Escape for thy life; look not behind thee, neither stay thou in all the plain; escape to the mountain, lest thou be consumed." Hesitancy or delay now would be fatal. To cast one lingering look upon the devoted city, to tarry for one moment from regret to leave so beautiful a home, would have cost their life. The storm of divine judgment was only waiting that these poor fugitives might make their escape.

But Lot, confused and terrified, pleaded that he could not do as he was required lest some evil should overtake him and he should die. Living in that wicked city, in the midst of unbelief, his faith had grown dim. The Prince of heaven was by his side, yet he pleaded for his own life as though God, who had manifested such care and love for him, would not still preserve him. He should have trusted himself wholly to the divine Messenger, giving his will and his life into the Lord's hands without a doubt or a question.

But like so many others, he endeavored to plan for himself: "Behold now, this city is near to flee unto, and it is a little one: O, let me escape thither, (is it not a little one?) and my soul shall live." The city here mentioned was Bela, afterward called Zoar. It was but a few miles from Sodom, and, like it, was corrupt and doomed to destruction. But Lot asked that it might be spared, urging that this was but a small request; and his desire was granted. The Lord assured him, "I have accepted thee concerning this thing also, that I will not overthrow this city, for the which thou hast spoken." Oh, how great the mercy of God toward His erring creatures!

Lot's Wife

Again the solemn command was given to hasten, for the fiery storm would be delayed but little longer. But one of the fugitives ventured to cast a look backward to the doomed city, and she became a monument of God's judgment. If Lot himself had manifested no hesitancy to obey the angels' warning, but had earnestly fled toward the mountains, without one word of pleading or remonstrance, his wife also would have made her escape. The influence of his example would have saved her from the sin that sealed her doom.

But his hesitancy and delay caused her to lightly regard the divine warning. While her body was upon the plain, her heart clung to Sodom, and she perished with it. She rebelled against God because His judgments involved her possessions and her children in the ruin.

Although so greatly favored in being called out from the wicked city, she felt that she was severely dealt with, because the wealth that it had taken years to accumulate must be left to destruction. Instead of thankfully accepting deliverance, she presumptuously looked back to desire the life of those who had rejected the divine warning. Her sin showed her to be unworthy of life, for the preservation of which she felt so little gratitude.

We should beware of treating lightly God's gracious provisions for our salvation. There are Christians who say, "I do not care to be saved unless my companion and children are saved with me." They feel that heaven would not be heaven to them without the presence of those who are so dear. But have those who cherish this feeling a right conception of their own relation to God, in view of His great goodness and mercy toward them? Have they forgotten that they are bound by the strongest ties of love and honor and loyalty to the service of their Creator and Redeemer?

The invitations of mercy are addressed to all; and because our friends reject the Saviour's pleading love, shall we also turn away? The redemption of the soul is precious. Christ has paid an infinite price for our salvation, and no one who appreciates the value of this great sacrifice or the worth of the soul will despise God's offered mercy because others choose to do so. The very fact that others are ignoring His just claims should arouse us to greater diligence, that we may honor God ourselves, and lead all whom we can influence, to accept His love.

Chapter 7

Based on Genesis 19.

Destruction By Fire

Destruction of Sodom—Part II

The sun was risen upon the earth when Lot entered into Zoar." The bright rays of the morning seemed to speak only prosperity and peace to the cities of the plain. The stir of active life began in the streets; men were going their various ways, intent on the business or the pleasures of the day. The sons-in-law of Lot were making merry at the fears and warnings of the weak-minded old man. Suddenly and unexpectedly as would be a thunder peal from an unclouded sky, the tempest broke.

The Lord rained brimstone and fire out of heaven upon the cities and the fruitful plain; its palaces and temples, costly dwellings, gardens and vineyards, and the gay [carefree or showy], pleasure-seeking throngs that only the night before had insulted the messengers of heaven—all were consumed. The smoke of the conflagration went up like the smoke of a great furnace. And the fair vale of Siddim became a desolation, a place never to be built up or inhabited—a witness to all generations of the certainty of God's judgments upon transgression.

The flames that consumed the cities of the plain shed their warning light down even to our time. We are taught the fearful and solemn lesson that while God's mercy bears long with the transgressor, there is a limit beyond which men may not go on in sin. When that limit is reached, then the offers of mercy are withdrawn, and the ministration of judgment begins.

Greater Sins than Sodom's

The Redeemer of the world declares that there are greater sins than that for which Sodom and Gomorrah were destroyed. Those who hear the gospel invitation calling sinners to repentance, and heed it not, are more guilty before God than were the dwellers in the vale of Siddim. And still greater sin is theirs who profess to know God and to keep His commandments, yet who deny Christ in their character and their daily life. In the light of the Saviour's warning, the fate of Sodom is a solemn admonition, not merely to those who are guilty of outbreaking sin, but to all who are trifling with Heaven-sent light and privileges.

Those who hear the gospel invitation calling sinners to repentance, and heed it not, are more guilty before God than were the dwellers in the vale of Siddim.

Said the True Witness to the church at Ephesus: "I have somewhat against thee, because thou hast left thy first love. Remember therefore from whence thou art fallen, and repent, and do the first works; or else I will come unto thee quickly, and will remove thy candlestick out of his place, except thou repent." Revelation 2:4, 5.

The Saviour watches for a response to His offers of love and forgiveness, with a more tender compassion than that which moves the heart of an earthly parent to forgive a wayward, suffering son. He cries after the wanderer, "Return unto Me, and I will return unto you." Malachi 3:7.

But if the erring one persistently refuses to heed the voice that calls him with pitying, tender love, he will at last be left in darkness. The heart that has long slighted God's mercy, becomes hardened in sin, and is no longer susceptible to the influence of the grace of God. Fearful will be the doom of that soul of whom the pleading Saviour shall finally declare, he "is joined to idols: let him alone." Hosea 4:17.

It will be more tolerable in the day of judgment for the cities of the plain than for those who have known the love of Christ, and yet have turned away to choose the pleasures of a world of sin.

You who are slighting the offers of mercy, think of the long array of figures accumulating against you in the books of heaven; for there is a record kept of the impieties of nations, of families, of individuals. God may bear long while the account goes on, and calls to repentance and offers of pardon may be given; yet a time will come when the account will be full; when the soul's decision has been made; when by his own choice man's destiny has been fixed. Then the signal will be given for judgment to be executed.

Lot's Day and Our Day

There is cause for alarm in the condition of the religious world today. God's mercy has been trifled with. The multitudes make void the law of Jehovah, "teaching for doctrines the commandments of men." Matthew 15:9.

Infidelity prevails in many of the churches in our land.

Infidelity prevails in many of the churches in our land; not infidelity in its broadest sense—an open denial of the Bible—but an infidelity that is robed in the garb of Christianity, while it is undermining faith in the Bible as a revelation from God. Fervent devotion and vital piety have given place to hollow formalism. As the result, apostasy and sensualism prevail. Christ declared, "As it was in the days of Lot, … even thus shall it be in the day when the Son of man is revealed." Luke 17:28, 30.

The daily record of passing events testifies to the fulfillment of His words. The world is fast becoming ripe for destruction. Soon the judgments of God are to be poured out, and sin and sinners are to be consumed.

Said our Saviour: "Take heed to yourselves, lest at any time your hearts be overcharged with surfeiting, and drunkenness, and cares of this life, and so that day come upon you unawares. For as a snare shall it come on all them that dwell on the face of the whole earth"—upon all whose interests are centered in this world. "Watch ye therefore, and pray always, that ye may be accounted worthy to escape all these things that shall come to pass, and to stand before the Son of man." Luke 21:34–36.

Before the destruction of Sodom, God sent a message to Lot, "Escape for thy life; look not behind thee, neither stay thou in all the plain; escape to the mountain, lest thou be consumed." The same voice of warning was heard by the disciples of Christ before the destruction of Jerusalem: "When ye shall see Jerusalem compassed with armies, then know that the desolation thereof is nigh. Then let them which are in Judea flee to the mountains." Luke 21:20, 21. They must not tarry to secure anything from their possessions, but must make the most of the opportunity to escape.

There was a coming out, a decided separation from the wicked, an escape for life. So it was in the days of Noah; so with Lot; so with the disciples prior to the destruction of Jerusalem; and so it will be in the last days. Again the voice of God is heard in a message of warning, bidding His people separate themselves from the prevailing iniquity.

So it was in the days of Noah; so with Lot; so with the disciples prior to the destruction of Jerusalem; and so it will be in the last days.

The state of corruption and apostasy that in the last days would exist in the religious world, was presented to the prophet John in the vision of Babylon, "that great city, which reigneth over the kings of the earth." Revelation 17:18. Before its destruction the call is to be given from heaven, "Come out of her, My people, that ye be not partakers of her sins, and that ye receive not of her plagues." Revelation 18:4.

As in the days of Noah and Lot, there must be a marked separation from sin and sinners. There can be no compromise between God and the world, no turning back to secure earthly treasures. "Ye cannot serve God and mammon." Matthew 6:24.

Like the dwellers in the vale of Siddim, the people are dreaming of prosperity and peace. "Escape for thy life," is the warning from the angels of God; but other voices are heard saying, "Be not excited;

there is no cause for alarm." The multitudes cry, "Peace and safety," while Heaven declares that swift destruction is about to come upon the transgressor.

On the night prior to their destruction, the cities of the plain rioted in pleasure and derided the fears and warnings of the messenger of God; but those scoffers perished in the flames; that very night the door of mercy was forever closed to the wicked, careless inhabitants of Sodom.

God will not always be mocked; He will not long be trifled with. "Behold, the day of the Lord cometh, cruel both with wrath and fierce anger, to lay the land desolate: and He shall destroy the sinners thereof out of it." Isaiah 13:9.

The great mass of the world will reject God's mercy, and will be overwhelmed in swift and irretrievable ruin. But those who heed the warning shall dwell "in the secret place of the Most High," and "abide under the shadow of the Almighty." His truth shall be their shield and buckler. For them is the promise, "With long life will I satisfy him, and show him My salvation." Psalm 91:1, 4, 16.

Lot dwelt but a short time in Zoar. Iniquity prevailed there as in Sodom, and he feared to remain, lest the city should be destroyed. Not long after, Zoar was consumed, as God had purposed. Lot made his way to the mountains, and abode in a cave, stripped of all for which he had dared to subject his family to the influences of a wicked city.

But the curse of Sodom followed him even here. The sinful conduct of his daughters was the result of the evil associations of that vile place. Its moral corruption had become so interwoven with their character that they could not distinguish between good and evil. Lot's only posterity, the Moabites and Ammonites, were vile, idolatrous tribes, rebels against God and bitter enemies of His people.

Contrasts Between Lives of Lot and Abraham

In how wide contrast to the life of Abraham was that of Lot! Once they had been companions, worshiping at one altar, dwelling side by side in their pilgrim tents; but how widely separated now!

Lot had chosen Sodom for its pleasure and profit. Leaving Abraham's altar and its daily sacrifice to the living God, he had permitted his children to mingle with a corrupt and idolatrous people; yet he had retained in his heart the fear of God, for he is declared in the Scriptures to have been a "just" man; his righteous soul was vexed with the vile conversation that greeted his ears daily and the violence and crime he was powerless to prevent.

He was saved at last as "a brand plucked out of the fire" (Zechariah 3:2), yet stripped of his possessions, bereaved of his wife and children, dwelling in caves, like the wild beasts, covered with infamy in his old age; and he gave to the world, not a race of righteous men, but two idolatrous nations, at enmity with God and warring upon His people, until, their cup of iniquity being full, they were appointed to destruction. How terrible were the results that followed one unwise step!

How terrible were the results that followed one unwise step!

Says the wise man, "Labor not to be rich: cease from thine own wisdom." "He that is greedy of gain troubleth his own house; but he that hateth gifts shall live." Proverbs 23:4; 15:27. And the apostle Paul declares, "They that will be rich fall into temptation and a snare, and into many foolish and hurtful lusts, which drown men in destruction and perdition." 1 Timothy 6:9.

When Lot entered Sodom he fully intended to keep himself free from iniquity and to command his household after him. But he signally failed. The corrupting influences about him had an effect upon his own faith, and his children's connection with the inhabitants of Sodom bound up his interest in a measure with theirs. The result is before us.

Mistakes in Selecting A Home

Many are still making a similar mistake. In selecting a home they look more to the temporal advantages they may gain than to the moral and social influences that will surround themselves and their families. They choose a beautiful and fertile country, or remove to some flourishing city, in the hope of securing greater prosperity; but their children are surrounded by temptation, and too often they form associations that are unfavorable to the development of piety and the formation of a right character.

The atmosphere of lax morality, of unbelief, of indifference to religious things, has a tendency to counteract the influence of the parents. Examples of rebellion against parental and divine authority are ever before the youth; many form attachments for infidels and unbelievers, and cast in their lot with the enemies of God.

Consider, first of all, the moral and religious influences that will surround us and our families.

In choosing a home, God would have us consider, first of all, the moral and religious influences that will surround us and our families. We may be placed in trying positions, for many cannot have their surroundings what they would; and whenever duty calls us, God will enable us to stand uncorrupted, if we watch and pray, trusting in the grace of Christ.

But we should not needlessly expose ourselves to influences that are unfavorable to the formation of Christian character. When we voluntarily place ourselves in an atmosphere of worldliness and unbelief, we displease God and drive holy angels from our homes.

Those who secure for their children worldly wealth and honor at the expense of their eternal interests, will find in the end that these advantages are a terrible loss. Like Lot, many see their children ruined, and barely save their own souls. Their lifework is lost; their life is a sad failure. Had they exercised true wisdom, their children might have had less of worldly prosperity, but they would have made sure of a title to the immortal inheritance.

Abraham's Example

The heritage that God has promised to His people is not in this world. Abraham had no possession in the earth, "no, not so much as to set his foot on." Acts 7:5. He possessed great substance, and he used it to the glory of God and the good of his fellow men; but he did not look upon this world as his home. The Lord had called him to leave his idolatrous countrymen, with the promise of the land of Canaan as an everlasting possession; yet neither he nor his son nor his son's son received it. When Abraham desired a burial place for his dead, he had to buy it of the Canaanites. His sole possession in the Land of Promise was that rock-hewn tomb in the cave of Machpelah.

God's promise may seem to be long delayed.

But the word of God had not failed; neither did it meet its final accomplishment in the occupation of Canaan by the Jewish people. "To Abraham and his seed were the promises made." Galatians 3:16. Abraham himself was to share the inheritance. The fulfillment of God's promise may seem to be long delayed—for "one day is with the Lord as a thousand years, and a thousand years as one day" (2 Peter 3:8); it may appear to tarry; but at the appointed time "it will surely come, it will not tarry." Habakkuk 2:3.

The gift to Abraham and his seed included not merely the land of Canaan, but the whole earth. So says the apostle, "The promise, that he should be the *heir of the world*, was not to Abraham, or to his seed, through the law, but through the righteousness of faith." Romans 4:13.

And the Bible plainly teaches that the promises made to Abraham are to be fulfilled through Christ. All that are Christ's are "Abraham's seed, and heirs according to the promise"—heirs to "an inheritance incorruptible, and undefiled, and that fadeth not away"—the earth freed from the curse of sin. Galatians 3:29; 1 Peter 1:4.

For "the kingdom and dominion, and the greatness of the kingdom under the whole heaven, shall be given to the people of the saints of the Most High;" and "the meek shall inherit the earth; and shall delight themselves in the abundance of peace." Daniel 7:27; Psalm 37:11.

God gave to Abraham a view of this immortal inheritance, and with this hope he was content. "By faith he sojourned in the Land of Promise, as in a strange country, dwelling in tabernacles with Isaac and Jacob, the heirs with him of the same promise: for he looked for a city which hath foundations, whose builder and maker is God." Hebrews 11:9, 10.

Of the posterity of Abraham it is written, "These all died in faith, not having received the promises, but having seen them afar off, and were persuaded of them, and embraced them, and confessed that they were strangers and pilgrims on the earth." Verse 13.

We must dwell as pilgrims and strangers here if we would gain "a better country, that is, an heavenly."

We must dwell as pilgrims and strangers here if we would gain "a better country, that is, an heavenly." Verse 16. Those who are children of Abraham will be seeking the city which he looked for, "whose builder and maker is God."

Chapter 8

Based on Matthew 24; Mark 13; Luke 21:5–38.

The Impending Doom

On the Mount of Olives—Part I

Christ's words to the priests and rulers, "Behold, your house is left unto you desolate" (Matthew 23:38), had struck terror to their hearts. They affected indifference, but the question kept rising in their minds as to the import of these words. An unseen danger seemed to threaten them. Could it be that the magnificent temple, which was the nation's glory, was soon to be a heap of ruins?

The foreboding of evil was shared by the disciples, and they anxiously waited for some more definite statement from Jesus. As they passed with Him out of the temple, they called His attention to its strength and beauty. The stones of the temple were of the purest marble, of perfect whiteness, and some of them of almost fabulous size. A portion of the wall had withstood the siege by Nebuchadnezzar's army. In its perfect masonry it appeared like one solid stone dug entire from the quarry. How those mighty walls could be overthrown the disciples could not comprehend.

In mercy to them He blended the description of the two great crises.

As Christ's attention was attracted to the magnificence of the temple, what must have been the unuttered thoughts of that Rejected One! The view before Him was indeed beautiful, but He said with sadness, I see it all. The buildings are indeed wonderful. You point to these walls as apparently indestructible; but listen to My words: The day will come when "there shall not be left one stone upon another, that shall not be thrown down."

Christ's words had been spoken in the hearing of a large number of people; but when He was alone, Peter, John, James, and Andrew came to Him as He sat upon the Mount of Olives. "Tell us," they said, "when shall these things be? and what shall be the sign of Thy coming, and of the end of the world?"

Jesus did not answer His disciples by taking up separately the destruction of Jerusalem and the great day of His coming. He mingled the description of these two events. Had He opened to His disciples future events as He beheld them, they would have been unable to endure the sight. In mercy to them He blended the description of the two great crises, leaving the disciples to study out the meaning for themselves.

When He referred to the destruction of Jerusalem, His prophetic words reached beyond that event to the final conflagration in that day when the Lord shall rise out of His place to punish the world for their iniquity, when the earth shall disclose her blood, and shall no more cover her slain.

This entire discourse was given, not for the disciples only, but for those who should live in the last scenes of this earth's history.

Signs of Jerusalem's Destruction

The same deceptions practiced prior to the destruction of Jerusalem have been practiced through the ages, and will be practiced again.

Turning to the disciples, Christ said, "Take heed that no man deceive you. For many shall come in My name, saying, I am Christ; and shall deceive many." Many false messiahs will appear, claiming to work miracles, and declaring that the time of the deliverance of the Jewish nation has come. These will mislead many.

Christ's words were fulfilled. Between His death and the siege of Jerusalem many false messiahs appeared. But this warning was given also to those who live in this age of the world. The same deceptions practiced prior to the destruction of Jerusalem have been practiced through the ages, and will be practiced again.

"And ye shall hear of wars and rumors of wars: see that ye be not troubled: for all these things must come to pass, but the end is not yet." Prior to the destruction of Jerusalem, men wrestled for the supremacy. Emperors were murdered. Those supposed to be standing next the throne were slain.

There were wars and rumors of wars. "All these things must come to pass," said Christ, "but the end [of the Jewish nation as a nation] is not yet. For nation shall rise against nation, and kingdom against kingdom: and there shall be famines, and pestilences, and earthquakes, in divers places. All these are the beginning of sorrows." Christ said.

As the rabbis see these signs, they will declare them to be God's judgments upon the nations for holding in bondage His chosen people. They will declare that these signs are the token of the advent of the Messiah. Be not deceived; they are the beginning of His judgments. The people have looked to themselves. They have not repented and been converted that I should heal them. The signs that they represent as tokens of their release from bondage are signs of their destruction.

"Then shall they deliver you up to be afflicted, and shall kill you: and ye shall be hated of all nations for My name's sake. And then shall many be offended, and shall betray one another, and shall hate one another." All this the Christians suffered. Fathers and mothers betrayed their children. Children betrayed their parents. Friends delivered their friends up to the Sanhedrin. The persecutors wrought out their purpose by killing Stephen, James, and other Christians.

God gave the Jewish people a last opportunity to repent.

Through His servants, God gave the Jewish people a last opportunity to repent. He manifested Himself through His witnesses in their arrest, in their trial, and in their imprisonment. Yet their judges pronounced on them the death sentence. They were men of whom the world was not worthy, and by killing them the Jews crucified afresh the Son of God.

So it will be again. The authorities will make laws to restrict religious liberty. They will assume the right that is God's alone. They will think they can force the conscience, which God alone should control. Even now they are making a beginning; this work they will continue to carry forward till they reach a boundary over which they cannot step. God will interpose in behalf of His loyal, commandment-keeping people.

The authorities will make laws to restrict religious liberty.

On every occasion when persecution takes place, those who witness it make decisions either for Christ or against Him. Those who manifest sympathy for the ones wrongly condemned show their attachment for Christ. Others are offended because the principles of truth cut directly across their practice. Many stumble and fall, apostatizing from the faith they once advocated. Those who apostatize in time of trial will, to secure their own safety, bear false witness, and betray their brethren. Christ has warned us of this, that we may not be surprised at the unnatural, cruel course of those who reject the light.

Christ gave His disciples a sign of the ruin to come on Jerusalem, and He told them how to escape: "When ye shall see Jerusalem compassed with armies, then know that the desolation thereof is nigh. Then let them which are in Judea flee to the mountains; and let them which are in the midst of it depart out; and let not them that are in the countries enter thereinto. For these be the days of vengeance, that all things which are written may be fulfilled."

This warning was given to be heeded forty years after, at the destruction of Jerusalem. The Christians obeyed the warning, and not a Christian perished in the fall of the city.

"Pray ye that your flight be not in the winter; neither on the Sabbath day," Christ said. He who made the Sabbath did not abolish it, nailing it to His cross. The Sabbath was not rendered null and void by His death. Forty years after His crucifixion it was still to be held sacred. For forty years the disciples were to pray that their flight might not be on the Sabbath day.

Signs of Christ's Second Coming

From the destruction of Jerusalem, Christ passed on rapidly to the greater event, the last link in the chain of this earth's history,—the coming of the Son of God in majesty and glory. Between these two events, there lay open to Christ's view long centuries of darkness, centuries for His church marked with blood and tears and agony. Upon these scenes His disciples could not then endure to look, and Jesus passed them by with a brief mention.

"Then shall be great tribulation," He said, "such as was not since the beginning of the world to this time, no, nor ever shall be. And except those days should be shortened, there should no flesh be saved: but for the elect's sake those days shall be shortened." For more than a thousand years such persecution as the world had never before known was to come upon Christ's followers. Millions upon millions of His faithful witnesses were to be slain. Had not God's hand been stretched out to preserve His people, all would have perished. "But for the elect's sake," He said, "those days shall be shortened."

In unmistakable language, our Lord speaks of His second coming.

Now, in unmistakable language, our Lord speaks of His second coming, and He gives warning of dangers to precede His advent to the world. "If any man shall say unto you, Lo, here is Christ, or there; believe it not. For there shall arise false christs, and false prophets, and shall show great signs and wonders; insomuch that, if it were possible, they shall deceive the very elect. Behold, I have told you before. Wherefore if they shall say unto you, Behold, He is in the desert; go not forth: behold, He is in the secret chambers; believe it not. For as the lightning cometh out of the east, and shineth even unto the west; so shall also the coming of the Son of man be."

As one of the signs of Jerusalem's destruction, Christ had said, "Many false prophets shall rise, and shall deceive many." False prophets did rise, deceiving the people, and leading great numbers into the desert. Magicians and sorcerers, claiming miraculous power, drew the people after them into the mountain solitudes. But this prophecy was spoken also for the last days. This sign is given as a sign of the second advent.

Even now false christs and false prophets are showing signs and wonders to seduce.

Even now false christs and false prophets are showing signs and wonders to seduce His disciples. Do we not hear the cry, "Behold, He is in the desert"? Have not thousands gone forth into the desert, hoping to find Christ?

And from thousands of gatherings where men profess to hold communion with departed spirits is not the call now heard, "Behold, He is in the secret chambers"? This is the very claim that spiritism puts forth. But what says Christ? "Believe it not. For as the lightning cometh out of the east, and shineth even unto the west; so shall also the coming of the Son of man be."

The Saviour gives signs of His coming, and more than this, He fixes the time when the first of these signs shall appear: "Immediately after the tribulation of those days shall the sun be darkened, and the moon shall not give her light, and the stars shall fall from heaven, and the powers of the heavens shall be shaken: and then shall appear the sign of the Son of man in heaven: and then shall all the tribes of the earth mourn, and they shall see the Son of man coming in the clouds of heaven with power and great glory. And He shall send His angels with a great sound of a trumpet, and they shall gather together His elect from the four winds, from one end of heaven to the other."

At the close of the great papal persecution, Christ declared, the sun should be darkened, and the moon should not give her light. Next, the stars should fall from heaven. And He says, "Learn a parable of the fig tree; When his branch is yet tender, and putteth forth leaves, ye know that summer is nigh: so likewise ye, when ye shall see all these things, know that He is near, even at the doors." Matthew 24:32, 33, margin.

Christ has given signs of His coming. He declares that we may know when He is near, even at the doors. He says of those who see these signs, "This generation shall not pass, till all these things be fulfilled." These signs have appeared. Now we know of a surety that the Lord's coming is at hand. "Heaven and earth shall pass away," He says, "but My words shall not pass away."

Christ is coming with clouds and with great glory. A multitude of shining angels will attend Him. He will come to raise the dead, and to change the living saints from glory to glory. He will come to honor those who have loved Him, and kept His commandments, and to take them to Himself. He has not forgotten them nor His promise. There will be a relinking of the family chain. When we look upon our dead, we may think of the morning when the trump of God shall sound, when "the dead shall be raised incorruptible, and we shall be changed." 1 Corinthians 15:52.

A little longer, and we shall see the King in His beauty. A little longer, and He will wipe all tears from our eyes. A little longer, and He will present us "faultless before the presence of His glory with exceeding joy." Jude 1:24. Wherefore, when He gave the signs of His coming He said, "When these things begin to come to pass, then look up, and lift up your heads; for your redemption draweth nigh."

A little longer, and we shall see the King in His beauty.

But the day and the hour of His coming Christ has not revealed. He stated plainly to His disciples that He Himself could not make known the day or the hour of His second appearing. Had He been at liberty to reveal this, why need He have exhorted them to maintain an attitude of constant expectancy?

There are those who claim to know the very day and hour of our Lord's appearing. Very earnest are they in mapping out the future. But the Lord has warned them off the ground they occupy. The exact time of the second coming of the Son of man is God's mystery.

Conditions At Christ's Coming

Christ continues, pointing out the condition of the world at His coming: "As the days of Noah were, so shall also the coming of the Son of man be. For as in the days that were before the Flood they were eating and drinking, marrying and giving in marriage, until the day that Noah entered into the ark, and knew not until the Flood came, and took them all away; so shall also the coming of the Son of man be."

Christ does not here bring to view a temporal millennium, a thousand years in which all are to prepare for eternity. He tells us that as it was in Noah's day, so will it be when the Son of man comes again.

How was it in Noah's day? "God saw that the wickedness of man was great in the earth, and that every imagination of the thoughts of his heart was only evil continually." Genesis 6:5. The inhabitants of the antediluvian world turned from Jehovah, refusing to do His holy will. They followed their own unholy imagination and perverted ideas. It was because of their wickedness that they were destroyed; and today the world is following the same way.

It presents no flattering signs of millennial glory. The transgressors of God's law are filling the earth with wickedness. Their betting, their horse racing, their gambling, their dissipation, their lustful practices, their untamable passions, are fast filling the world with violence.

In the prophecy of Jerusalem's destruction Christ said, "Because iniquity shall abound, the love of many shall wax cold. But he that shall endure unto the end, the same shall be saved. And this gospel of the kingdom shall be preached in all the world for a witness unto all nations; and then shall the end come."

Before the coming of the Son of man, the everlasting gospel is to be preached.

This prophecy will again be fulfilled. The abounding iniquity of that day finds its counterpart in this generation. So with the prediction in regard to the preaching of the gospel. Before the fall of Jerusalem, Paul, writing by the Holy Spirit, declared that the gospel was preached to "every creature which is under heaven." Colossians 1:23.

So now, before the coming of the Son of man, the everlasting gospel is to be preached "to every nation, and kindred, and tongue, and people." Revelation 14:6, 14.

God "hath appointed a day, in the which He will judge the world." Acts 17:31. Christ tells us when that day shall be ushered in. He does not say that all the world will be converted, but that "this gospel of the kingdom shall be preached in all the world for a witness unto all nations; and then shall the end come." By giving the gospel to the world it is in our power to hasten our Lord's return. We are not only to look for but to hasten the coming of the day of God. 2 Peter 3:12, margin.

Had the church of Christ done her appointed work as the Lord ordained, the whole world would before this have been warned, and the Lord Jesus would have come to our earth in power and great glory.

Chapter 9

Based on Matthew 24; Mark 13: Luke 21:5–38.

Take Heed!

On the Mount of Olives—Part II

After He had given the signs of His coming, Christ said, "When ye see these things come to pass, know ye that the kingdom of God is nigh at hand." "Take ye heed, watch and pray." God has always given men warning of coming judgments. Those who had faith in His message for their time, and who acted out their faith, in obedience to His commandments, escaped the judgments that fell upon the disobedient and unbelieving.

God has always given men warning of coming judgments.

The word came to Noah, "Come thou and all thy house into the ark; for thee have I seen righteous before Me." Noah obeyed and was saved. The message came to Lot, "Up, get you out of this place; for the Lord will destroy this city." Genesis 7:1; 19:14. Lot placed himself under the guardianship of the heavenly messengers, and was saved.

So Christ's disciples were given warning of the destruction of Jerusalem. Those who watched for the sign of the coming ruin, and fled from the city, escaped the destruction. So now we are given warning of Christ's second coming and of the destruction to fall upon the world. Those who heed the warning will be saved.

Watch for the Lord's Coming

Because we know not the exact time of His coming, we are commanded to watch. "Blessed are those servants, whom the Lord when He cometh shall find watching." Luke 12:37.

Those who watch for the Lord's coming are not waiting in idle expectancy. The expectation of Christ's coming is to make men fear the Lord, and fear His judgments upon transgression. It is to awaken them to the great sin of rejecting His offers of mercy.

Those who watch for the Lord's coming are not waiting in idle expectancy.

Those who are watching for the Lord are purifying their souls by obedience to the truth. With vigilant watching they combine earnest working. Because they know that the Lord is at the door, their zeal is quickened to co-operate with the divine intelligences in working for the salvation of souls. These are the faithful and wise servants who give to the Lord's household "their portion of meat in due season." Luke 12:42. They are declaring the truth that is now specially applicable. As Enoch, Noah, Abraham, and Moses each declared the truth for his time, so will Christ's servants now give the special warning for their generation.

But Christ brings to view another class: "If that evil servant shall say in his heart, My lord delayeth his coming; and shall begin to smite his fellow servants, and to eat and drink with the drunken; the lord of that servant shall come in a day when he looketh not for him."

The Evil Servant

The evil servant says in his heart, "My lord delayeth his coming." He does not say that Christ will not come. He does not scoff at the idea of His second coming. But in his heart and by his actions and words he declares that the Lord's coming is delayed. He banishes from the minds of others the conviction that the Lord is coming quickly. His influence leads men to presumptuous, careless delay. They are confirmed in their worldliness and stupor. Earthly passions, corrupt thoughts, take possession of the mind.

The evil servant eats and drinks with the drunken, unites with the world in pleasure seeking. He smites his fellow servants, accusing and condemning those who are faithful to their Master. He mingles with the world. Like grows with like in transgression. It is a fearful assimilation. With the world he is taken in the snare. "The lord of that servant shall come … in an hour that he is not aware of, and shall cut him asunder, and appoint him his portion with the hypocrites."

"If therefore thou shalt not watch, I will come on thee as a thief, and thou shalt not know what hour I will come upon thee." Revelation 3:3. The advent of Christ will surprise the false teachers. They are saying, "Peace and safety." Like the priests and teachers before the fall of Jerusalem, they look for the church to enjoy earthly prosperity and glory. The signs of the times they interpret as foreshadowing this. But what saith the word of Inspiration? "Sudden destruction cometh upon them." 1 Thessalonians 5:3.

Upon all who make this world their home, the day of God will come as a snare.

Upon all who dwell on the face of the whole earth, upon all who make this world their home, the day of God will come as a snare. It comes to them as a prowling thief.

The world, full of rioting, full of godless pleasure, is asleep, asleep in carnal security. Men are putting afar off the coming of the Lord. They laugh at warnings. The proud boast is made, "All things continue as they were from the beginning." "Tomorrow shall be as this day, and much more abundant." 2 Peter 3:4; Isaiah 56:12. We will go deeper into pleasure loving. But Christ says, "Behold, I come as a thief." Revelation 16:15.

At the very time when the world is asking in scorn, "Where is the promise of His coming?" the signs are fulfilling. While they cry, "Peace and safety," sudden destruction is coming. When the scorner, the rejecter of truth, has become presumptuous; when the routine of work in the various money-making lines is carried on without regard to principle; when the student is eagerly seeking knowledge of everything but his Bible, Christ comes as a thief.

Everything in the world is in agitation. The signs of the times are ominous. Coming events cast their shadows before. The Spirit of God is withdrawing from the earth, and calamity follows calamity by sea and by land. There are tempests, earthquakes, fires, floods, murders of every grade. Who can read the future? Where is security? There is assurance in nothing that is human or earthly. Rapidly are men ranging themselves under the banner they have chosen. Restlessly are they waiting and watching the movements of their leaders.

Everything in the world is in agitation. The signs of the times are ominous.

There are those who are waiting and watching and working for our Lord's appearing. Another class are falling into line under the generalship of the first great apostate. Few believe with heart and soul that we have a hell to shun and a heaven to win.

The crisis is stealing gradually upon us. The sun shines in the heavens, passing over its usual round, and the heavens still declare the glory of God. Men are still eating and drinking, planting and building, marrying, and giving in marriage. Merchants are still buying and selling. Men are jostling one against another, contending for the highest place. Pleasure lovers are still crowding to theaters, horse races, gambling hells. The highest excitement prevails, yet probation's hour is fast closing, and every case is about to be eternally decided.

Satan sees that his time is short. He has set all his agencies at work that men may be deceived, deluded, occupied and entranced, until the day of probation shall be ended, and the door of mercy be forever shut.

Solemnly there come to us down through the centuries the warning words of our Lord from the Mount of Olives: "Take heed to yourselves, lest at any time your hearts be overcharged with surfeiting, and drunkenness, and cares of this life, and so that day come upon you unawares." "Watch ye therefore, and pray always, that ye may be accounted worthy to escape all these things that shall come to pass, and to stand before the Son of man."

Part 3

Thought Questions

- *What fundamental questions about God's character are raised by the destruction in the days of Noah and Lot?*
- *How did sin originate? Why does a good God allow evil and suffering in the world?*
- *How does God balance His justice and mercy? How did His dealings with Lucifer shed light on His dealings with all sinners?*
- *How will God eventually destroy sin and sinners, and how will true peace and harmony be eventually restored?*
- *How will God finally be justified in executing judgment upon sin? What assurance is given for future happiness?*
- *How will the cross of Christ be regarded throughout the ages? What mysteries will be ever unfolding in its light?*

The Problem of Evil

"On the day you were created."

"How you are fallen from heaven, O Lucifer, son of the morning! How you are cut down to the ground, you who weakened the nations! For you have said in your heart: 'I will ascend into heaven, I will exalt my throne above the stars of God; I will also sit on the mount of the congregation on the farthest sides of the north; I will ascend above the heights of the clouds, I will be like the Most High. Yet you shall be brought down to Sheol, To the lowest depths of the Pit." (Isaiah 14:12–15 NKJV)

"You were the seal of perfection, full of wisdom and perfect in beauty. You were in Eden, the garden of God; every precious stone was your covering: … The workmanship of your timbrels and pipes was prepared for you ***on the day you were created****. "You were the anointed cherub who covers; I established you; You were on the holy mountain of God; you walked back and forth in the midst of fiery stones. You were perfect in your ways from the day you were created, till [the day] iniquity was found in you." (Ezekiel 28:12–15 NKJV, emphasis added)*

But the day of the Lord will come as a thief in the night, in which the heavens will pass away with a great noise, and the elements will melt with fervent heat; both the earth and the works that are in it will be burned up… Nevertheless we, according to His promise, look for new heavens and a new earth in which righteousness dwells. (2 Peter 3:10–13 NKJV)

Chapter 10

Based on Isaiah 14:12–21; Ezekiel 28:1–19.

Why Was Sin Permitted?

The Origin of Evil

To many minds the origin of sin and the reason for its existence are a source of great perplexity. They see the work of evil, with its terrible results of woe and desolation, and they question how all this can exist under the sovereignty of One who is infinite in wisdom, in power, and in love. Here is a mystery of which they find no explanation. And in their uncertainty and doubt they are blinded to truths plainly revealed in God's word and essential to salvation.

There are those who, in their inquiries concerning the existence of sin, endeavor to search into that which God has never revealed; hence they find no solution of their difficulties; and such as are actuated by a disposition to doubt and cavil seize upon this as an excuse for rejecting the words of Holy Writ.

Others, however, fail of a satisfactory understanding of the great problem of evil, from the fact that tradition and misinterpretation have obscured the teaching of the Bible concerning the character of God, the nature of His government, and the principles of His dealing with sin.

Sin, An Intruder

It is impossible to explain the origin of sin so as to give a reason for its existence. Yet enough may be understood concerning both the origin and the final disposition of sin to make fully manifest the justice and benevolence of God in all His dealings with evil.

Nothing is more plainly taught in Scripture than that God was in no wise responsible for the entrance of sin; that there was no arbitrary withdrawal of divine grace, no deficiency in the divine government, that gave occasion for the uprising of rebellion.

Sin is an intruder, for whose presence no reason can be given. It is mysterious, unaccountable; to excuse it is to defend it. Could excuse for it be found, or cause be shown for its existence, it would cease to be sin.

Sin is an intruder, for whose presence no reason can be given.

Our only definition of sin is that given in the word of God; it is "the transgression of the law;" it is the outworking of a principle at war with the great law of love which is the foundation of the divine government.

Before the entrance of evil there was peace and joy throughout the universe. All was in perfect harmony with the Creator's will. Love for God was supreme, love for one another impartial. Christ the Word, the Only Begotten of God, was one with the eternal Father,—one in nature, in character, and in purpose,—the only being in all the universe that could enter into all the counsels and purposes of God.

By Christ the Father wrought in the creation of all heavenly beings. "By Him were all things created, that are in heaven, … whether they be thrones, or dominions, or principalities, or powers" (Colossians 1:16); and to Christ, equally with the Father, all heaven gave allegiance.

The law of love being the foundation of the government of God, the happiness of all created beings depended upon their perfect accord with its great principles of righteousness. God desires from all His creatures the service of love—homage that springs from an intelligent appreciation of His character. He takes no pleasure in a forced allegiance, and to all He grants freedom of will, that they may render Him voluntary service.

Lucifer's Note of Discord

But there was one that chose to pervert this freedom. Sin originated with him who, next to Christ, had been most honored of God and who stood highest in power and glory among the inhabitants of heaven.

Before his fall, Lucifer was first of the covering cherubs, holy and undefiled. "Thus saith the Lord God; Thou sealest up the sum, full of wisdom, and perfect in beauty. Thou hast been in Eden the garden of God; every precious stone was thy covering. … Thou art the anointed cherub that covereth; and I have set thee so: thou wast upon the holy mountain of God; thou hast walked up and down in the midst of the stones of fire. Thou wast perfect in thy ways from the day that thou wast created, till iniquity was found in thee." Ezekiel 28:12–15.

Lucifer might have remained in favor with God, beloved and honored by all the angelic host, exercising his noble powers to bless others and to glorify his Maker. But, says the prophet, "Thine heart was lifted up because of thy beauty, thou hast corrupted thy wisdom by reason of thy brightness." Verse 17.

Little by little, Lucifer came to indulge a desire for self- exaltation.

Little by little, Lucifer came to indulge a desire for self-exaltation. "Thou hast set thine heart as the heart of God." "Thou hast said, … I will exalt my throne above the stars of God: I will sit also upon the mount of the congregation. … I will ascend above the heights of the clouds; I will be like the Most High." Verse 6; Isaiah 14:13, 14.

Instead of seeking to make God supreme in the affections and allegiance of His creatures, it was Lucifer's endeavor to win their service and homage to himself. And coveting the honor which the infinite Father had bestowed upon His Son, this prince of angels aspired to power which it was the prerogative of Christ alone to wield.

All heaven had rejoiced to reflect the Creator's glory and to show forth His praise. And while God was thus honored, all had been peace and gladness. But a note of discord now marred the celestial harmonies. The service and exaltation of self, contrary to the Creator's plan, awakened forebodings of evil in minds to whom God's glory was supreme.

The heavenly councils pleaded with Lucifer. The Son of God presented before him the greatness, the goodness, and the justice of the Creator, and the sacred, unchanging nature of His law. God Himself had established the order of heaven; and in departing from it, Lucifer would dishonor his Maker, and bring ruin upon himself. But the warning, given in infinite love and mercy, only aroused a spirit of resistance. Lucifer allowed jealousy of Christ to prevail, and he became the more determined.

Pride in his own glory nourished the desire for supremacy. The high honors conferred upon Lucifer were not appreciated as the gift of God and called forth no gratitude to the Creator. He gloried in his brightness and exaltation, and aspired to be equal with God. He was beloved and reverenced by the heavenly host. Angels delighted to execute his commands, and he was clothed with wisdom and glory above them all.

Yet the Son of God was the acknowledged Sovereign of heaven, one in power and authority with the Father. In all the councils of God, Christ was a participant, while Lucifer was not permitted thus to enter into the divine purposes. "Why," questioned this mighty angel, "should Christ have the supremacy? Why is He thus honored above Lucifer?"

Leaving his place in the immediate presence of God, Lucifer went forth to diffuse the spirit of discontent among the angels. Working with mysterious secrecy, and for a time concealing his real purpose under an appearance of reverence for God, he endeavored to excite dissatisfaction concerning the laws that governed heavenly beings, intimating that they imposed an unnecessary restraint. Since their natures were holy, he urged that the angels should obey the dictates of their own will.

He sought to create sympathy for himself by representing that God had dealt unjustly with him in bestowing supreme honor upon Christ. He claimed that in aspiring to greater power and honor he was not aiming at self-exaltation, but was seeking to secure liberty for all the inhabitants of heaven, that by this means they might attain to a higher state of existence.

God's Mercy and Forbearance

God in His great mercy bore long with Lucifer.

God in His great mercy bore long with Lucifer. He was not immediately degraded from his exalted station when he first indulged the spirit of discontent, nor even when he began to present his false claims before the loyal angels. Long was he retained in heaven.

Again and again he was offered pardon on condition of repentance and submission. Such efforts as only infinite love and wisdom could devise were made to convince him of his error. The spirit of discontent had never before been known in heaven. Lucifer himself did not at first see whither he was drifting; he did not understand the real nature of his feelings. But as his dissatisfaction was proved to be without cause, Lucifer was convinced that he was in the wrong, that the divine claims were just, and that he ought to acknowledge them as such before all heaven. Had he done this, he might have saved himself and many angels.

He had not at this time fully cast off his allegiance to God. Though he had forsaken his position as covering cherub, yet if he had been willing to return to God, acknowledging the Creator's wisdom, and satisfied to fill the place appointed him in God's great plan, he would have been reinstated in his office. But pride forbade him to submit. He persistently defended his own course, maintained that he had no need of repentance, and fully committed himself, in the great controversy, against his Maker.

All the powers of his master mind were now bent to the work of deception, to secure the sympathy of the angels that had been under his command. Even the fact that Christ had warned and counseled him was perverted to serve his traitorous designs.

To those whose loving trust bound them most closely to him, Satan had represented that he was wrongly judged, that his position was not respected, and that his liberty was to be abridged.

From misrepresentation of the words of Christ he [Lucifer] passed to prevarication and direct falsehood, accusing the Son of God of a design to humiliate him before the inhabitants of heaven.

He sought also to make a false issue between himself and the loyal angels. All whom he could not subvert and bring fully to his side he accused of indifference to the interests of heavenly beings. The very work which he himself was doing he charged upon those who remained true to God. And to sustain his charge of God's injustice toward him, he resorted to misrepresentation of the words and acts of the Creator.

From misrepresentation of the words of Christ he [Lucifer] passed to prevarication and direct falsehood.

It was his policy to perplex the angels with subtle arguments concerning the purposes of God. Everything that was simple he shrouded in mystery, and by artful perversion cast doubt upon the plainest statements of Jehovah. His high position, in such close connection with the divine administration, gave greater force to his representations, and many were induced to unite with him in rebellion against Heaven's authority.

God in His wisdom permitted Satan to carry forward his work, until the spirit of disaffection ripened into active revolt. It was necessary for his plans to be fully developed, that their true nature and tendency might be seen by all. Lucifer, as the anointed cherub, had been highly exalted; he was greatly loved by the heavenly beings, and his influence over them was strong.

God's government included not only the inhabitants of heaven, but of all the worlds that He had created; and Satan thought that if he could carry the angels of heaven with him in rebellion, he could carry also the other worlds. He had artfully presented his side of the question, employing sophistry and fraud to secure his objects. His power to deceive was very great, and by disguising himself in a cloak of falsehood he had gained an advantage. Even the loyal angels could not fully discern his character or see to what his work was leading.

Satan had been so highly honored, and all his acts were so clothed with mystery, that it was difficult to disclose to the angels the true nature of his work. Until fully developed, sin would not appear the evil thing it was. Heretofore it had had no place in the universe of God,

Until fully developed, sin would not appear the evil thing it was.

and holy beings had no conception of its nature and malignity. They could not discern the terrible consequences that would result from setting aside the divine law.

Satan had, at first, concealed his work under a specious profession of loyalty to God. He claimed to be seeking to promote the honor of God, the stability of His government, and the good of all the inhabitants of heaven. While instilling discontent into the minds of the angels under him, he had artfully made it appear that he was seeking to remove dissatisfaction. When he urged that changes be made in the order and laws of God's government, it was under the pretense that these were necessary in order to preserve harmony in heaven.

Sin Given Time To Reveal Itself

In His dealing with sin, God could employ only righteousness and truth. Satan could use what God could not—flattery and deceit. He had sought to falsify the word of God and had misrepresented His plan of government before the angels, claiming that God was not just in laying laws and rules upon the inhabitants of heaven; that in requiring submission and obedience from His creatures, He was seeking merely the exaltation of Himself.

Therefore it must be demonstrated before the inhabitants of heaven, as well as of all the worlds, that God's government was just, His law perfect. Satan had made it appear that he himself was seeking to promote the good of the universe. The true character of the usurper, and his real object, must be understood by all. He must have time to manifest himself by his wicked works.

The discord which his own course had caused in heaven, Satan charged upon the law and government of God. All evil he declared to be the result of the divine administration. He claimed that it was his own object to improve upon the statutes of Jehovah. Therefore it was necessary that he should demonstrate the nature of his claims, and show the working out of his proposed changes in the divine law. His own work must condemn him. Satan had claimed from the first that he was not in rebellion. The whole universe must see the deceiver unmasked.

Even when it was decided that he could no longer remain in heaven, Infinite Wisdom did not destroy Satan. Since the service of love can alone be acceptable to God, the allegiance of His creatures must rest upon a conviction of His justice and benevolence. The inhabitants of heaven and of other worlds, being unprepared to comprehend the nature or consequences of sin, could not then have seen the justice and mercy of God in the destruction of Satan.

Had he been immediately blotted from existence, they would have served God from fear rather than from love. The influence of the deceiver would not have been fully destroyed, nor would the spirit of rebellion have been utterly eradicated.

Evil must be permitted to come to maturity.

Evil must be permitted to come to maturity. For the good of the entire universe through ceaseless ages Satan must more fully develop his principles, that his charges against the divine government might be seen in their true light by all created beings, that the justice and mercy of God and the immutability of His law might forever be placed beyond all question.

Satan's rebellion was to be a lesson to the universe through all coming ages, a perpetual testimony to the nature and terrible results of sin. The working out of Satan's rule, its effects upon both men and angels, would show what must be the fruit of setting aside the divine authority. It would testify that with the existence of God's government and His law is bound up the well-being of all the creatures He has made. Thus the history of this terrible experiment of rebellion was to be a perpetual safeguard to all holy intelligences, to prevent them from being deceived as to the nature of transgression, to save them from committing sin and suffering its punishments.

Lucifer's Spirit of Self-Justification

To the very close of the controversy in heaven the great usurper continued to justify himself. When it was announced that with all his sympathizers he must be expelled from the abodes of bliss, then the rebel leader boldly avowed his contempt for the Creator's law. He reiterated his claim that angels needed no control, but should be left to follow their own will, which would ever guide them right. He denounced the divine statutes as a restriction of their liberty and declared that it was his purpose to secure the abolition of law; that, freed from this restraint, the hosts of heaven might enter upon a more exalted, more glorious state of existence.

With one accord, Satan and his host threw the blame of their rebellion wholly upon Christ, declaring that if they had not been reproved, they would never have rebelled. Thus stubborn and defiant in their disloyalty, seeking vainly to overthrow the government of God, yet blasphemously claiming to be themselves the innocent victims of oppressive power, the archrebel and all his sympathizers were at last banished from heaven.

The same spirit that prompted rebellion in heaven still inspires rebellion on earth.

The same spirit that prompted rebellion in heaven still inspires rebellion on earth. Satan has continued with men the same policy which he pursued with the angels. His spirit now reigns in the children of disobedience. Like him they seek to break down the restraints of the law of God and promise men liberty through transgression of its precepts.

Reproof of sin still arouses the spirit of hatred and resistance. When God's messages of warning are brought home to the conscience, Satan leads men to justify themselves and to seek the sympathy of others in their course of sin. Instead of correcting their errors, they excite indignation against the reprover, as if he were the sole cause of difficulty. From the days of righteous Abel to our own time such is the spirit which has been displayed toward those who dare to condemn sin.

By the same misrepresentation of the character of God as he had practiced in heaven, causing Him to be regarded as severe and tyrannical, Satan induced man to sin. And having succeeded thus far, he declared that God's unjust restrictions had led to man's fall, as they had led to his own rebellion.

But the Eternal One Himself proclaims His character: "The Lord God, merciful and gracious, long-suffering, and abundant in goodness and truth, keeping mercy for thousands, forgiving iniquity and transgression and sin, and that will by no means clear the guilty." Exodus 34:6, 7.

In the atonement the character of God is revealed.

In the banishment of Satan from heaven, God declared His justice and maintained the honor of His throne. But when man had sinned through yielding to the deceptions of this apostate spirit, God gave an evidence of His love by yielding up His only-begotten Son to die for the fallen race. In the atonement the character of God is revealed. The mighty argument of the cross demonstrates to the whole universe that the course of sin which Lucifer had chosen was in no wise chargeable upon the government of God.

The Great Controversy

In the contest between Christ and Satan, during the Saviour's earthly ministry, the character of the great deceiver was unmasked. Nothing could so effectually have uprooted Satan from the affections of the heavenly angels and the whole loyal universe as did his cruel warfare upon the world's Redeemer.

The daring blasphemy of his [Satan's] demand that Christ should pay him homage, his presumptuous boldness in bearing Him to the mountain summit and the pinnacle of the temple, the malicious intent betrayed in urging Him to cast Himself down from the dizzy height, the unsleeping malice that hunted Him from place to place, inspiring the hearts of priests and people to reject His love, and at the last to cry, "Crucify Him! crucify Him!"—all this excited the amazement and indignation of the universe.

It was Satan that prompted the world's rejection of Christ. The prince of evil exerted all his power and cunning to destroy Jesus; for he saw that the Saviour's mercy and love, His compassion and pitying tenderness, were representing to the world the character of God.

Satan contested every claim put forth by the Son of God and employed men as his agents to fill the Saviour's life with suffering and sorrow. The sophistry and falsehood by which he had sought to hinder the work of Jesus, the hatred manifested through the children of disobedience, his cruel accusations against Him whose life was one of unexampled goodness, all sprang from deep-seated revenge. The pent-up fires of envy and malice, hatred and revenge, burst forth on Calvary against the Son of God, while all heaven gazed upon the scene in silent horror.

The pent-up fires of envy and malice, hatred and revenge, burst forth on Calvary against the Son of God.

When the great sacrifice had been consummated, Christ ascended on high, refusing the adoration of angels until He had presented the request: "I will that they also, whom Thou hast given Me, be with Me where I am." John 17:24. Then with inexpressible love and power came forth the answer from the Father's throne: "Let all the angels of God worship Him." Hebrews 1:6. Not a stain rested upon Jesus. His humiliation ended, His sacrifice completed, there was given unto Him a name that is above every name.

Now the guilt of Satan stood forth without excuse. He had revealed his true character as a liar and a murderer. It was seen that the very same spirit with which he ruled the children of men, who were under his power, he would have manifested had he been permitted to control the inhabitants of heaven. He had claimed that the transgression of God's law would bring liberty and exaltation; but it was seen to result in bondage and degradation.

Satan's lying charges against the divine character and government appeared in their true light. He had accused God of seeking merely the exaltation of Himself in requiring submission and obedience from His creatures, and had declared that, while the Creator exacted self-denial from all others, He Himself practiced no self-denial and made no sacrifice.

Now it was seen that for the salvation of a fallen and sinful race, the Ruler of the universe had made the greatest sacrifice which love could make; for "God was in Christ, reconciling the world unto Himself." 2 Corinthians 5:19. It was seen, also, that while Lucifer had opened the door for the entrance of sin by his desire for honor and supremacy, Christ had, in order to destroy sin, humbled Himself and become obedient unto death.

God had manifested His abhorrence of the principles of rebellion. All heaven saw His justice revealed, both in the condemnation of Satan and in the redemption of man. Lucifer had declared that if the law of God was changeless, and its penalty could not be remitted, every transgressor must be forever debarred from the Creator's favor. He had claimed that the sinful race were placed beyond redemption and were therefore his rightful prey.

But the death of Christ was an argument in man's behalf that could not be overthrown. The penalty of the law fell upon Him who was equal with God, and man was free to accept the righteousness of Christ and by a life of penitence and humiliation to triumph, as the Son of God had triumphed, over the power of Satan. Thus God is just and yet the justifier of all who believe in Jesus.

But it was not merely to accomplish the redemption of man that Christ came to the earth to suffer and to die. He came to "magnify the law" and to "make it honorable." Not alone that the inhabitants of this world might regard the law as it should be regarded; but it was to demonstrate to all the worlds of the universe that God's law is unchangeable.

Could its claims have been set aside, then the Son of God need not have yielded up His life to atone for its transgression. The death of Christ proves it immutable. And the sacrifice to which infinite love impelled the Father and the Son, that sinners might be redeemed, demonstrates to all the universe—what nothing less than this plan of atonement could have sufficed to do—that justice and mercy are the foundation of the law and government of God.

How It Will All End

In the final execution of the judgment it will be seen that no cause for sin exists. When the Judge of all the earth shall demand of Satan, "Why hast thou rebelled against Me, and robbed Me of the subjects of My kingdom?" the originator of evil can render no excuse. Every mouth will be stopped, and all the hosts of rebellion will be speechless.

The cross of Calvary, while it declares the law immutable, proclaims to the universe that the wages of sin is death. In the Saviour's expiring cry, "It is finished," the death knell of Satan was rung. The great controversy which had been so long in progress was then decided, and the final eradication of evil was made certain. The Son of God passed through the portals of the tomb, that "through death He might destroy him that had the power of death, that is, the devil." Hebrews 2:14.

Lucifer's desire for self-exaltation had led him to say: "I will exalt my throne above the stars of God: ... I will be like the Most High." God declares: "I will bring thee to ashes upon the earth, ... and never shalt thou be any more." Isaiah 14:13, 14; Ezekiel 28:18, 19.

When "the day cometh, that shall burn as an oven; ... all the proud, yea, and all that do wickedly, shall be stubble: and the day that cometh shall burn them up, saith the Lord of hosts, that it shall leave them neither root nor branch." Malachi 4:1.

The whole universe will have become witnesses to the nature and results of sin. And its utter extermination, which in the beginning would have brought fear to angels and dishonor to God, will now vindicate His love and establish His honor before the universe of beings who delight to do His will, and in whose heart is His law.

Never will evil again be manifest. Says the word of God: "Affliction shall not rise up the second time." Nahum 1:9. The law of God, which Satan has reproached as the yoke of bondage, will be honored as the law of liberty. A tested and proved creation will never again be turned from allegiance to Him whose character has been fully manifested before them as fathomless love and infinite wisdom.

Chapter 11

Based on Revelation 19 and 22.

God's Power at Midnight

God's People Delivered—Part I

In this chapter and the next ones, the author has woven together many scriptural passages to paint a vivid picture of the world's closing scenes, culminating in the glorious coming of Christ, the destruction of the wicked, and the deliverance of God's people.

—The Publishers

When the protection of human laws shall be withdrawn from those who honor the law of God, there will be, in different lands, a simultaneous movement for their destruction. As the time appointed in the decree draws near, the people will conspire to root out the hated sect. It will be determined to strike in one night a decisive blow, which shall utterly silence the voice of dissent and reproof.

The people of God—some in prison cells, some hidden in solitary retreats in the forests and the mountains—still plead for divine protection, while in every quarter companies of armed men, urged on by hosts of evil angels, are preparing for the work of death. It is now, in the hour of utmost extremity, that the God of Israel will interpose for the deliverance of His chosen.

Saith the Lord; "Ye shall have a song, as in the night when a holy solemnity is kept; and gladness of heart, as when one goeth ... to come into the mountain of the Lord, to the Mighty One of Israel. And the Lord shall cause His glorious voice to be heard, and shall show the lighting down of His arm, with the indignation of His anger, and with the flame of a devouring fire, with scattering, and tempest, and hailstones." Isaiah 30:29, 30.

Deliverance At Midnight

With shouts of triumph, jeering, and imprecation, throngs of evil men are about to rush upon their prey, when, lo, a dense blackness, deeper than the darkness of the night, falls upon the earth. Then a rainbow, shining with the glory from the throne of God, spans the heavens and seems to encircle each praying company. The angry multitudes are suddenly arrested. Their mocking cries die away. The objects of their murderous rage are forgotten. With fearful forebodings they gaze upon the symbol of God's covenant and long to be shielded from its overpowering brightness.

By the people of God a voice, clear and melodious, is heard, saying, "Look up," and lifting their eyes to the heavens, they behold the bow of promise. The black, angry clouds that covered the firmament are parted, and like Stephen they look up steadfastly into heaven and see the glory of God and the Son of man seated upon His throne. In His divine form they discern the marks of His humiliation; and from His lips they hear the request presented before His Father and the holy angels: "I will that they also, whom Thou hast given Me, be with Me where I am." John 17:24.

Again a voice, musical and triumphant, is heard, saying: "They come! they come! holy, harmless, and undefiled. They have kept the word of My patience; they shall walk among the angels;" and the pale, quivering lips of those who have held fast their faith utter a shout of victory.

Everything in nature seems turned out of its course.

It is at midnight that God manifests His power for the deliverance of His people. The sun appears, shining in its strength. Signs and wonders follow in quick succession. The wicked look with terror and amazement upon the scene, while the righteous behold with solemn joy the tokens of their deliverance. Everything in nature seems turned out of its course. The streams cease to flow. Dark, heavy clouds come up and clash against each other. In the midst of the angry heavens is one clear space of indescribable glory, whence comes the voice of God like the sound of many waters, saying: "It is done." Revelation 16:17.

That voice shakes the heavens and the earth. There is a mighty earthquake, "such as was not since men were upon the earth, so mighty an earthquake, and so great." Verses 17, 18. The firmament appears to open and shut. The glory from the throne of God seems flashing through. The mountains shake like a reed in the wind, and ragged rocks are scattered on every side. There is a roar as of a coming tempest. The sea is lashed into fury. There is heard the shriek of a hurricane like the voice of demons upon a mission of destruction.

The whole earth heaves and swells like the waves of the sea. Its surface is breaking up. Its very foundations seem to be giving way. Mountain chains are sinking. Inhabited islands disappear. The seaports that have become like Sodom for wickedness are swallowed up by the angry waters. Babylon the great has come in remembrance before God, "to give unto her the cup of the wine of the fierceness of His wrath." Great hailstones, every one "about the weight of a talent," are doing their work of destruction. Verses 19, 21.

The proudest cities of the earth are laid low. The lordly palaces, upon which the world's great men have lavished their wealth in order to glorify themselves, are crumbling to ruin before their eyes. Prison walls are rent asunder, and God's people, who have been held in bondage for their faith, are set free.

Graves are opened, and "many of them that sleep in the dust of the earth… awake, some to everlasting life, and some to shame and everlasting contempt." Daniel 12:2. All who have died in the faith of the third angel's message come forth from the tomb glorified, to hear God's covenant of peace with those who have kept His law. "They also which pierced Him" (Revelation 1:7), those that mocked and derided Christ's dying agonies, and the most violent opposers of His truth and His people, are raised to behold Him in His glory and to see the honor placed upon the loyal and obedient.

Thick clouds still cover the sky; yet the sun now and then breaks through, appearing like the avenging eye of Jehovah. Fierce lightnings leap from the heavens, enveloping the earth in a sheet of flame. Above the terrific roar of thunder, voices, mysterious and awful, declare the doom of the wicked. The words spoken are not comprehended by all; but they are distinctly understood by the false teachers. Those who a little before were so reckless, so boastful and defiant, so exultant in their cruelty to God's commandment-keeping people, are now overwhelmed with consternation and shuddering in fear. Their wails are heard above the sound of the elements. Demons acknowledge the deity of Christ and tremble before His power, while men are supplicating for mercy and groveling in abject terror.

Said the prophets of old, as they beheld in holy vision the day of God: "Howl ye; for the day of the Lord is at hand; it shall come as a destruction from the Almighty." Isaiah 13:6. "Enter into the rock, and hide thee in the dust, for fear of the Lord, and for the glory of His majesty. The lofty looks of man shall be humbled, and the haughtiness of men shall be bowed down, and the Lord alone shall be exalted in that day. For the day of the Lord of hosts shall be upon everyone that is proud and lofty, and upon everyone that is lifted up; and he shall be brought low." "In that day a man shall cast the idols of his silver, and the idols of his gold, which they made each one for himself to worship, to the moles and to the bats; to go into the clefts of the rocks, and into the tops of the ragged rocks, for fear of the Lord, and for the glory of His majesty, when He ariseth to shake terribly the earth." Isaiah 2:10–12, 20, 21, margin.

The Holy Law: The Standard of Judgment

Through a rift in the clouds there beams a star whose brilliancy is increased fourfold in contrast with the darkness. It speaks hope and joy to the faithful, but severity and wrath to the transgressors of God's law. Those who have sacrificed all for Christ are now secure, hidden as in the secret of the Lord's pavilion. They have been tested, and before the world and the despisers of truth they have evinced their fidelity to Him who died for them.

God is our refuge and strength, a very present help in trouble.

A marvelous change has come over those who have held fast their integrity in the very face of death. They have been suddenly delivered from the dark and terrible tyranny of men transformed to demons. Their faces, so lately pale, anxious, and haggard, are now aglow with wonder, faith, and love. Their voices rise in triumphant song: "God is our refuge and strength, a very present help in trouble. Therefore will not we fear, though the earth be removed, and though the mountains be carried into the midst of the sea; though the waters thereof roar and be troubled, though the mountains shake with the swelling thereof." Psalm 46:1–3.

While these words of holy trust ascend to God, the clouds sweep back, and the starry heavens are seen, unspeakably glorious in contrast with the black and angry firmament on either side. The glory of the celestial city streams from the gates ajar. Then there appears against the sky a hand holding two tables of stone folded together. Says the prophet: "The heavens shall declare His righteousness: for God is judge Himself." Psalm 50:6.

That holy law, God's righteousness, that amid thunder and flame was proclaimed from Sinai as the guide of life, is now revealed to men as the rule of judgment. The hand opens the tables, and there are seen the precepts of the Decalogue, traced as with a pen of fire. The words are so plain that all can read them. Memory is aroused, the darkness of superstition and heresy is swept from every mind, and God's ten words, brief, comprehensive, and authoritative, are presented to the view of all the inhabitants of the earth.

It is impossible to describe the horror and despair of those who have trampled upon God's holy requirements. The Lord gave them His law; they might have compared their characters with it and learned their defects while there was yet opportunity for repentance and reform; but in order to secure the favor of the world, they set aside its precepts and taught others to transgress. They have endeavored to compel God's people to profane His Sabbath. Now they are condemned by that law which they have despised.

With awful distinctness they see that they are without excuse. They chose whom they would serve and worship. "Then shall ye return, and discern between the righteous and the wicked, between him that serveth God and him that serveth Him not." Malachi 3:18.

The enemies of God's law, from the ministers down to the least among them, have a new conception of truth and duty. Too late they see that the Sabbath of the fourth commandment is the seal of the living God. Too late they see the true nature of their spurious sabbath and the sandy foundation upon which they have been building. They find that they have been fighting against God.

Religious teachers have led souls to perdition while professing to guide them to the gates of Paradise. Not until the day of final accounts will it be known how great is the responsibility of men in holy office and how terrible are the results of their unfaithfulness. Only in eternity can we rightly estimate the loss of a single soul. Fearful will be the doom of him to whom God shall say: Depart, thou wicked servant.

Not until the day of final accounts will it be known how great is the responsibility of men in holy office and how terrible are the results of their unfaithfulness.

The voice of God is heard from heaven, declaring the day and hour of Jesus' coming, and delivering the everlasting covenant to His people. Like peals of loudest thunder His words roll through the earth. The Israel of God stand listening, with their eyes fixed upward. Their countenances are lighted up with His glory, and shine as did the face of Moses when he came down from Sinai. The wicked cannot look upon them. And when the blessing is pronounced on those who have honored God by keeping His Sabbath holy, there is a mighty shout of victory.

The King of Kings Descends

Soon there appears in the east a small black cloud, about half the size of a man's hand. It is the cloud which surrounds the Saviour and which seems in the distance to be shrouded in darkness. The people of God know this to be the sign of the Son of man. In solemn silence they gaze upon it as it draws nearer the earth, becoming lighter and more glorious, until it is a great white cloud, its base a glory like consuming fire, and above it the rainbow of the covenant.

Jesus rides forth as a mighty conqueror. Not now a "Man of Sorrows," to drink the bitter cup of shame and woe, He comes, victor in heaven and earth, to judge the living and the dead. "Faithful and True," "in righteousness He doth judge and make war." And "the armies which were in heaven" (Revelation 19:11, 14) follow Him. With anthems of celestial melody the holy angels, a vast, unnumbered throng, attend Him on His way. The firmament seems filled with radiant forms—"ten thousand times ten thousand, and thousands of thousands."

No human pen can portray the scene; no mortal mind is adequate to conceive its splendor.

No human pen can portray the scene; no mortal mind is adequate to conceive its splendor. "His glory covered the heavens, and the earth was full of His praise. And His brightness was as the light." Habakkuk 3:3, 4.

As the living cloud comes still nearer, every eye beholds the Prince of life. No crown of thorns now mars that sacred head; but a diadem of glory rests on His holy brow. His countenance outshines the dazzling brightness of the noonday sun. "And He hath on His vesture and on His thigh a name written, *King of kings, and Lord of lords.*" Revelation 19:16.

Before His presence "all faces are turned into paleness;" upon the rejecters of God's mercy falls the terror of eternal despair. "The heart melteth, and the knees smite together, ... and the faces of them all gather blackness." Jeremiah 30:6; Nahum 2:10. The righteous cry with trembling: "Who shall be able to stand?" The angels' song is hushed, and there is a period of awful silence. Then the voice of Jesus is heard, saying: "My grace is sufficient for you." The faces of the righteous are lighted up, and joy fills every heart. And the angels strike a note higher and sing again as they draw still nearer to the earth.

The King of kings descends upon the cloud, wrapped in flaming fire. The heavens are rolled together as a scroll, the earth trembles before Him, and every mountain and island is moved out of its place. "Our God shall come, and shall not keep silence: a fire shall devour before Him, and it shall be very tempestuous round about Him. He shall call to the heavens from above, and to the earth, that He may judge His people." Psalm 50:3, 4.

"And the kings of the earth, and the great men, and the rich men, and the chief captains, and the mighty men, and every bondman, and every freeman, hid themselves in the dens and in the rocks of the mountains; and said to the mountains and rocks, Fall on us, and hide us from the face of Him that sitteth on the throne, and from the wrath of the Lamb: for the great day of His wrath is come; and who shall be able to stand?" Revelation 6:15–17.

The derisive jests have ceased. Lying lips are hushed into silence. The clash of arms, the tumult of battle, "with confused noise, and garments rolled in blood" (Isaiah 9:5), is stilled. Nought now is heard but the voice of prayer and the sound of weeping and lamentation. The cry bursts forth from lips so lately scoffing: "The great day of His wrath is come; and who shall be able to stand?" The wicked pray to be buried beneath the rocks of the mountains rather than meet the face of Him whom they have despised and rejected.

That voice which penetrates the ear of the dead, they know. How often have its plaintive, tender tones called them to repentance. How often has it been heard in the touching entreaties of a friend, a brother, a Redeemer. To the rejecters of His grace no other could be so full of condemnation, so burdened with denunciation, as that voice which has so long pleaded: "Turn ye, turn ye from your evil ways; for why will ye die?" Ezekiel 33:11. Oh, that it were to them the voice of a stranger! Says Jesus: "I have called, and ye refused; I have stretched out My hand, and no man regarded; but ye have set at nought all My counsel, and would none of My reproof." Proverbs 1:24, 25. That voice awakens memories which they would fain blot out—warnings despised, invitations refused, privileges slighted.

Those who derided His claim to be the Son of God are speechless now.

There are those who mocked Christ in His humiliation. With thrilling power come to their minds the Sufferer's words, when, adjured by the high priest, He solemnly declared: "Hereafter shall ye see the Son of man sitting on the right hand of power, and coming in the clouds of heaven." Matthew 26:64. Now they behold Him in His glory, and they are yet to see Him sitting on the right hand of power.

Those who derided His claim to be the Son of God are speechless now. There is the haughty Herod who jeered at His royal title and bade the mocking soldiers crown Him king. There are the very men who with impious hands placed upon His form the purple robe, upon His sacred brow the thorny crown, and in His unresisting hand the mimic scepter, and bowed before Him in blasphemous mockery. The men who smote and spit upon the Prince of life now turn from His piercing gaze and seek to flee from the overpowering glory of His presence. Those who drove the nails through His hands and feet, the soldier who pierced His side, behold these marks with terror and remorse.

With awful distinctness do priests and rulers recall the events of Calvary. With shuddering horror they remember how, wagging their heads in satanic exultation, they exclaimed: "He saved others; Himself He cannot save. If He be the King of Israel, let Him now come down from the cross, and we will believe Him. He trusted in God; let Him deliver Him now, if He will have Him." Matthew 27:42, 43.

Vividly they recall the Saviour's parable of the husbandmen who refused to render to their lord the fruit of the vineyard, who abused his servants and slew his son. They remember, too, the sentence which they themselves pronounced: The lord of the vineyard "will miserably destroy those wicked men."

In the sin and punishment of those unfaithful men the priests and elders see their own course and their own just doom. And now there rises a cry of mortal agony. Louder than the shout, "Crucify Him, crucify Him," which rang through the streets of Jerusalem, swells the awful, despairing wail, "He is the Son of God! He is the true Messiah!" They seek to flee from the presence of the King of kings. In the deep caverns of the earth, rent asunder by the warring of the elements, they vainly attempt to hide.

In the lives of all who reject truth there are moments when conscience awakens.

In the lives of all who reject truth there are moments when conscience awakens, when memory presents the torturing recollection of a life of hypocrisy and the soul is harassed with vain regrets. But what are these compared with the remorse of that day when "fear cometh as desolation," when "destruction cometh as a whirlwind"! Proverbs 1:27. Those who would have destroyed Christ and His faithful people now witness the glory which rests upon them. In the midst of their terror they hear the voices of the saints in joyful strains exclaiming: "Lo, this is our God; we have waited for Him, and He will save us." Isaiah 25:9.

Chapter 12

Based on Revelation 19 and 22.

The Final Deliverance

God's People Delivered—Part II

Amid the reeling of the earth, the flash of lightning, and the roar of thunder, the voice of the Son of God calls forth the sleeping saints. He looks upon the graves of the righteous, then, raising His hands to heaven, He cries: "Awake, awake, awake, ye that sleep in the dust, and arise!"

Throughout the length and breadth of the earth the dead shall hear that voice, and they that hear shall live. And the whole earth shall ring with the tread of the exceeding great army of every nation, kindred, tongue, and people. From the prison house of death they come, clothed with immortal glory, crying: "O death, where is thy sting? O grave, where is thy victory?" 1 Corinthians 15:55. And the living righteous and the risen saints unite their voices in a long, glad shout of victory.

The Glorious Resurrection

All come forth from their graves the same in stature as when they entered the tomb. Adam, who stands among the risen throng, is of lofty height and majestic form, in stature but little below the Son of God. He presents a marked contrast to the people of later generations; in this one respect is shown the great degeneracy of the race. But all arise with the freshness and vigor of eternal youth.

In the beginning, man was created in the likeness of God, not only in character, but in form and feature. Sin defaced and almost obliterated the divine image; but Christ came to restore that which had been lost. He will change our vile bodies and fashion them like unto His glorious body. The mortal, corruptible form, devoid of comeliness, once

Oh, wonderful redemption! long talked of, long hoped for, contemplated with eager anticipation, but never fully understood.

polluted with sin, becomes perfect, beautiful, and immortal. All blemishes and deformities are left in the grave. Restored to the tree of life in the long-lost Eden, the redeemed will "grow up" (Malachi 4:2) to the full stature of the race in its primeval glory. The last lingering traces of the curse of sin will be removed, and Christ's faithful ones will appear in "the beauty of the Lord our God," in mind and soul and body reflecting the perfect image of their Lord. Oh, wonderful redemption! long talked of, long hoped for, contemplated with eager anticipation, but never fully understood.

The living righteous are changed "in a moment, in the twinkling of an eye." At the voice of God they were glorified; now they are made immortal and with the risen saints are caught up to meet their Lord in the air. Angels "gather together His elect from the four winds, from one end of heaven to the other." Little children are borne by holy angels to their mothers' arms. Friends long separated by death are united, nevermore to part, and with songs of gladness ascend together to the City of God.

On each side of the cloudy chariot are wings, and beneath it are living wheels; and as the chariot rolls upward, the wheels cry, "Holy," and the wings, as they move, cry, "Holy," and the retinue of angels cry, "Holy, holy, holy, Lord God Almighty." And the redeemed shout, "Alleluia!" as the chariot moves onward toward the New Jerusalem.

The Welcome Into the Holy City

Before entering the City of God, the Saviour bestows upon His followers the emblems of victory and invests them with the insignia of their royal state. The glittering ranks are drawn up in the form of a hollow square about their King, whose form rises in majesty high above saint and angel, whose countenance beams upon them full of benignant love.

Throughout the unnumbered host of the redeemed every glance is fixed upon Him, every eye beholds His glory whose "visage was so marred more than any man, and His form more than the sons of men." Upon the heads of the overcomers, Jesus with His own right hand places the crown of glory. For each there is a crown, bearing his own "new name" (Revelation 2:17), and the inscription, "Holiness to the Lord."

In every hand are placed the victor's palm and the shining harp. Then, as the commanding angels strike the note, every hand sweeps the harp strings with skillful touch, awaking sweet music in rich, melodious strains. Rapture unutterable thrills every heart, and each voice is raised in grateful praise: "Unto Him that loved us, and washed us from our sins in His own blood, and hath made us kings and priests unto God and His Father; to Him be glory and dominion for ever and ever." Revelation 1:5, 6.

Before the ransomed throng is the Holy City. Jesus opens wide the pearly gates, and the nations that have kept the truth enter in. There they behold the Paradise of God, the home of Adam in his innocency. Then that voice, richer than any music that ever fell on mortal ear, is heard, saying: "Your conflict is ended." "Come, ye blessed of My Father, inherit the kingdom prepared for you from the foundation of the world."

Now is fulfilled the Saviour's prayer for His disciples: "I will that they also, whom Thou hast given Me, be with Me where I am." "Faultless before the presence of His glory with exceeding joy" (Jude 24), Christ presents to the Father the purchase of His blood, declaring: "Here am I, and the children whom Thou hast given Me." "Those that Thou gavest Me I have kept."

Oh, the wonders of redeeming love!

Oh, the wonders of redeeming love! the rapture of that hour when the infinite Father, looking upon the ransomed, shall behold His image, sin's discord banished, its blight removed, and the human once more in harmony with the divine!

With unutterable love, Jesus welcomes His faithful ones to the joy of their Lord. The Saviour's joy is in seeing, in the kingdom of glory, the souls that have been saved by His agony and humiliation. And the redeemed will be sharers in His joy, as they behold, among the blessed, those who have been won to Christ through their prayers, their labors, and their loving sacrifice.

As they gather about the great white throne, gladness unspeakable will fill their hearts, when they behold those whom they have won for Christ, and see that one has gained others, and these still others, all brought into the haven of rest, there to lay their crowns at Jesus' feet and praise Him through the endless cycles of eternity.

The Reunion of the Two Adams

As the ransomed ones are welcomed to the City of God, there rings out upon the air an exultant cry of adoration. The two Adams are about to meet. The Son of God is standing with outstretched arms to receive the father of our race—the being whom He created, who sinned against his Maker, and for whose sin the marks of the crucifixion are borne upon the Saviour's form.

As Adam discerns the prints of the cruel nails, he does not fall upon the bosom of his Lord, but in humiliation casts himself at His feet, crying: "Worthy, worthy is the Lamb that was slain!" Tenderly the Saviour lifts him up and bids him look once more upon the Eden home from which he has so long been exiled.

After his expulsion from Eden, Adam's life on earth was filled with sorrow. Every dying leaf, every victim of sacrifice, every blight upon the fair face of nature, every stain upon man's purity, was a fresh reminder of his sin.

Terrible was the agony of remorse as he beheld iniquity abounding, and, in answer to his warnings, met the reproaches cast upon himself as the cause of sin. With patient humility he bore, for nearly a thousand years, the penalty of transgression. Faithfully did he repent of his sin and trust in the merits of the promised Saviour, and he died in the hope of a resurrection. The Son of God redeemed man's failure and fall; and now, through the work of the atonement, Adam is reinstated in his first dominion.

Adam is reinstated in his first dominion.

Transported with joy, he beholds the trees that were once his delight—the very trees whose fruit he himself had gathered in the days of his innocence and joy. He sees the vines that his own hands have trained, the very flowers that he once loved to care for. His mind grasps the reality of the scene; he comprehends that this is indeed Eden restored, more lovely now than when he was banished from it.

The Saviour leads him to the tree of life and plucks the glorious fruit and bids him eat. He looks about him and beholds a multitude of his family redeemed, standing in the Paradise of God. Then he casts his glittering crown at the feet of Jesus and, falling upon His breast, embraces the Redeemer. He touches the golden harp, and the vaults of heaven echo the triumphant song: "Worthy, worthy, worthy is the Lamb that was slain, and lives again!" The family of Adam take up the strain and cast their crowns at the Saviour's feet as they bow before Him in adoration.

This reunion is witnessed by the angels who wept at the fall of Adam and rejoiced when Jesus, after His resurrection, ascended to heaven, having opened the grave for all who should believe on His name. Now they behold the work of redemption accomplished, and they unite their voices in the song of praise.

Upon the crystal sea before the throne, that sea of glass as it were mingled with fire,—so resplendent is it with the glory of God,—are gathered the company that have "gotten the victory over the beast, and over his image, and over his mark, and over the number of his name." With the Lamb upon Mount Zion, "having the harps of God," they stand, the hundred and forty and four thousand that were redeemed from among men; and there is heard, as the sound of many waters, and as the sound of a great thunder, "the voice of harpers harping with their harps."

And they sing "a new song" before the throne, a song which no man can learn save the hundred and forty and four thousand. It is the song of Moses and the Lamb—a song of deliverance. None but the hundred and forty-four thousand can learn that song; for it is the song of their experience—an experience such as no other company have ever had.

"These are they which follow the Lamb whithersoever He goeth." These, having been translated from the earth, from among the living, are counted as "the first fruits unto God and to the Lamb." Revelation 15:2, 3; 14:1–5. "These are they which came out of great tribulation;" they have passed through the time of trouble such as never was since there was a nation; they have endured the anguish of the time of Jacob's trouble; they have stood without an intercessor through the final outpouring of God's judgments.

But they have been delivered, for they have "washed their robes, and made them white in the blood of the Lamb." "In their mouth was found no guile: for they are without fault" before God. "Therefore are they before the throne of God, and serve Him day and night in His temple: and He that sitteth on the throne shall dwell among them." They have seen the earth wasted with famine and pestilence, the sun having power to scorch men with great heat, and they themselves have endured suffering, hunger, and thirst. But "they shall hunger no more, neither thirst any more; neither shall the sun light on them, nor any heat. For the Lamb which is in the midst of the throne shall feed them, and shall lead them unto living fountains of waters: and God shall wipe away all tears from their eyes." Revelation 7:14–17.

In all ages the Saviour's chosen have been educated and disciplined in the school of trial.

In all ages the Saviour's chosen have been educated and disciplined in the school of trial. They walked in narrow paths on earth; they were purified in the furnace of affliction. For Jesus' sake they endured opposition, hatred, calumny. They followed Him through conflicts sore; they endured self-denial and experienced bitter disappointments. By their own painful experience they learned the evil of sin, its power, its guilt, its woe; and they look upon it with abhorrence.

A sense of the infinite sacrifice made for its cure humbles them in their own sight and fills their hearts with gratitude and praise which those who have never fallen cannot appreciate. They love much because they have been forgiven much. Having been partakers of Christ's sufferings, they are fitted to be partakers with Him of His glory.

The heirs of God have come from garrets, from hovels, from dungeons, from scaffolds, from mountains, from deserts, from the caves of the earth, from the caverns of the sea. On earth they were "destitute, afflicted, tormented." Millions went down to the grave loaded with infamy because they steadfastly refused to yield to the deceptive claims of

Satan. By human tribunals they were adjudged the vilest of criminals. But now "God is judge Himself." Psalm 50:6.

Now the decisions of earth are reversed. "The rebuke of His people shall He take away."Isaiah 25:8. "They shall call them, The holy people, The redeemed of the Lord." He hath appointed "to give unto them beauty for ashes, the oil of joy for mourning, the garment of praise for the spirit of heaviness." Isaiah 62:12; 61:3.

They are no longer feeble, afflicted, scattered, and oppressed. Henceforth they are to be ever with the Lord. They stand before the throne clad in richer robes than the most honored of the earth have ever worn. They are crowned with diadems more glorious than were ever placed upon the brow of earthly monarchs.

The days of pain and weeping are forever ended.

The days of pain and weeping are forever ended. The King of glory has wiped the tears from all faces; every cause of grief has been removed. Amid the waving of palm branches they pour forth a song of praise, clear, sweet, and harmonious; every voice takes up the strain, until the anthem swells through the vaults of heaven: "Salvation to our God which sitteth upon the throne, and unto the Lamb." And all the inhabitants of heaven respond in the ascription: "Amen: Blessing, and glory, and wisdom, and thanksgiving, and honor, and power, and might, be unto our God for ever and ever." Revelation 7:10, 12.

The Theme of Redemption

In this life we can only begin to understand the wonderful theme of redemption. With our finite comprehension we may consider most earnestly the shame and the glory, the life and the death, the justice and the mercy, that meet in the cross; yet with the utmost stretch of our mental powers we fail to grasp its full significance. The length and the breadth, the depth and the height, of redeeming love are but dimly comprehended.

The plan of redemption will not be fully understood, even when the ransomed see as they are seen and know as they are known; but through the eternal ages new truth will continually unfold to the wondering and delighted mind. Though the griefs and pains and temptations of earth are ended and the cause removed, the people of God will ever have a distinct, intelligent knowledge of what their salvation has cost.

The cross of Christ will be the science and the song of the redeemed through all eternity. In Christ glorified they will behold Christ crucified. Never will it be forgotten that He whose power created and upheld the unnumbered worlds through the vast realms of space, the Beloved of God, the Majesty of heaven, He whom cherub and shining seraph delighted to adore—humbled Himself to uplift fallen man; that He bore the guilt and shame of sin, and the hiding of His Father's face, till the woes of a lost world broke His heart and crushed out His life on Calvary's cross. That the Maker of all worlds, the Arbiter of all destinies, should lay aside His glory and humiliate Himself from love to man will ever excite the wonder and adoration of the universe.

The mystery of the cross explains all other mysteries.

As the nations of the saved look upon their Redeemer and behold the eternal glory of the Father shining in His countenance; as they behold His throne, which is from everlasting to everlasting, and know that His kingdom is to have no end, they break forth in rapturous song: "Worthy, worthy is the Lamb that was slain, and hath redeemed us to God by His own most precious blood!"

The mystery of the cross explains all other mysteries. In the light that streams from Calvary the attributes of God which had filled us with fear and awe appear beautiful and attractive. Mercy, tenderness, and parental love are seen to blend with holiness, justice, and power.

While we behold the majesty of His throne, high and lifted up, we see His character in its gracious manifestations, and comprehend, as never before, the significance of that endearing title, "Our Father."

It will be seen that He who is infinite in wisdom could devise no plan for our salvation except the sacrifice of His Son. The compensation for this sacrifice is the joy of peopling the earth with ransomed beings, holy, happy, and immortal. The result of the Saviour's conflict with the powers of darkness is joy to the redeemed, redounding to the glory of God throughout eternity. And such is the value of the soul that the Father is satisfied with the price paid; and Christ Himself, beholding the fruits of His great sacrifice, is satisfied.

Chapter 13

Based on Revelation 20 and 21.

The Pulse of Harmony

The Controversy Ended

"I saw a new heaven and a new earth: for the first heaven and the first earth were passed away." Revelation 21:1. The fire that consumes the wicked purifies the earth. Every trace of the curse is swept away. No eternally burning hell will keep before the ransomed the fearful consequences of sin.

One reminder alone remains: Our Redeemer will ever bear the marks of His crucifixion. Upon His wounded head, upon His side, His hands and feet, are the only traces of the cruel work that sin has wrought. Says the prophet, beholding Christ in His glory: "He had bright beams coming out of His side: and there was the hiding of His power." Habakkuk 3:4, margin.

That pierced side whence flowed the crimson stream that reconciled man to God—there is the Saviour's glory, there "the hiding of His power." "Mighty to save," through the sacrifice of redemption, He was therefore strong to execute justice upon them that despised God's mercy. And the tokens of His humiliation are His highest honor; through the eternal ages the wounds of Calvary will show forth His praise and declare His power.

"O Tower of the flock, the stronghold of the daughter of Zion, unto Thee shall it come, even the first dominion." Micah 4:8. The time has come to which holy men have looked with longing since the flaming sword barred the first pair from Eden, the time for "the redemption of the purchased possession." Ephesians 1:14. The earth originally given to man as his kingdom, betrayed by him into the hands of Satan, and so long held by the mighty foe, has been brought back by the great plan of redemption.

All that was lost by sin has been restored. "Thus saith the Lord … that formed the earth and made it; He hath established it, He created it not in vain, He formed it to be inhabited." Isaiah 45:18. God's original purpose in the creation of the earth is fulfilled as it is made the eternal abode of the redeemed. "The righteous shall inherit the land, and dwell therein forever." Psalm 37:29.

The Heavenly Home

A fear of making the future inheritance seem too material has led many to spiritualize away the very truths which lead us to look upon it as our home. Christ assured His disciples that He went to prepare mansions for them in the Father's house. Those who accept the teachings of God's word will not be wholly ignorant concerning the heavenly abode.

And yet, "eye hath not seen, nor ear heard, neither have entered into the heart of man, the things which God hath prepared for them that love Him." 1 Corinthians 2:9. Human language is inadequate to describe the reward of the righteous. It will be known only to those who behold it. No finite mind can comprehend the glory of the Paradise of God.

No finite mind can comprehend the glory of the Paradise of God.

In the Bible the inheritance of the saved is called "a country." Hebrews 11:14–16. There the heavenly Shepherd leads His flock to fountains of living waters. The tree of life yields its fruit every month, and the leaves of the tree are for the service of the nations. There are ever-flowing streams, clear as crystal, and beside them waving trees cast their shadows upon the paths prepared for the ransomed of the Lord. There the wide-spreading plains swell into hills of beauty, and the mountains of God rear their lofty summits. On those peaceful plains, beside those living streams, God's people, so long pilgrims and wanderers, shall find a home.

"My people shall dwell in a peaceable habitation, and in sure dwellings, and in quiet resting places." "Violence shall no more be heard in thy land, wasting nor destruction within thy borders; but thou shalt call thy walls Salvation, and thy gates Praise." "They shall build houses, and inhabit them; and they shall plant vineyards, and eat the fruit of them. They shall not build, and another inhabit; they shall not plant, and another eat: ... Mine elect shall long enjoy the work of their hands." Isaiah 32:18; 60:18; Isaiah 65:21, 22.

There, "the wilderness and the solitary place shall be glad for them; and the desert shall rejoice, and blossom as the rose." "Instead of the thorn shall come up the fir tree, and instead of the brier shall come up the myrtle tree." "The wolf also shall dwell with the lamb, and the leopard shall lie down with the kid; ... and a little child shall lead them." "They shall not hurt nor destroy in all My holy mountain," saith the Lord. Isaiah 35:1; 55:13; Isaiah 11:6, 9.

Pain cannot exist in the atmosphere of heaven. There will be no more tears, no funeral trains, no badges of mourning.

Pain cannot exist in the atmosphere of heaven. There will be no more tears, no funeral trains, no badges of mourning. "There shall be no more death, neither sorrow, nor crying: ... for the former things are passed away." "The inhabitant shall not say, I am sick: the people that dwell therein shall be forgiven their iniquity." Revelation 21:4; Isaiah 33:24.

The City of God

There is the New Jerusalem, the metropolis of the glorified new earth, "a crown of glory in the hand of the Lord, and a royal diadem in the hand of thy God." "Her light was like unto a stone most precious, even like a jasper stone, clear as crystal." "The nations of them which are saved shall walk in the light of it: and the kings of the earth do bring their glory and honor into it." Saith the Lord: "I will rejoice in Jerusalem, and joy in My people." "The tabernacle of God is with men, and He will dwell with them, and they shall be His people, and God Himself shall be with them, and be their God." Isaiah 62:3; Revelation 21:11, 24; Isaiah 65:19; Revelation 21:3.

In the City of God "there shall be no night." None will need or desire repose. There will be no weariness in doing the will of God and offering praise to His name. We shall ever feel the freshness of the morning and shall ever be far from its close. "And they need no candle, neither light of the sun; for the Lord God giveth them light." Revelation 22:5.

The light of the sun will be superseded by a radiance which is not painfully dazzling, yet which immeasurably surpasses the brightness of our noontide. The glory of God and the Lamb floods the Holy City with unfading light. The redeemed walk in the sunless glory of perpetual day.

"I saw no temple therein: for the Lord God Almighty and the Lamb are the temple of it." Revelation 21:22. The people of God are privileged to hold open communion with the Father and the Son. "Now we see through a glass, darkly." 1 Corinthians 13:12. We behold the image of God reflected, as in a mirror, in the works of nature and in His dealings with men; but then we shall see Him face to face, without a dimming veil between. We shall stand in His presence and behold the glory of His countenance.

Every faculty will be developed, every capacity increased.

There the redeemed shall know, even as also they are known. The loves and sympathies which God Himself has planted in the soul shall there find truest and sweetest exercise. The pure communion with holy beings, the harmonious social life with the blessed angels and with the faithful ones of all ages who have washed their robes and made them white in the blood of the Lamb, the sacred ties that bind together "the whole family in heaven and earth" (Ephesians 3:15)—these help to constitute the happiness of the redeemed.

There, immortal minds will contemplate with never-failing delight the wonders of creative power, the mysteries of redeeming love. There will be no cruel, deceiving foe to tempt to forgetfulness of God. Every faculty will be developed, every capacity increased. The acquirement of knowledge will not weary the mind or exhaust the energies. There the grandest enterprises may be carried forward, the loftiest aspirations reached, the highest ambitions realized; and still there will arise new heights to surmount, new wonders to admire, new truths to comprehend, fresh objects to call forth the powers of mind and soul and body.

All the treasures of the universe will be open to the study of God's redeemed. Unfettered by mortality, they wing their tireless flight to worlds afar—worlds that thrilled with sorrow at the spectacle of human woe and rang with songs of gladness at the tidings of a ransomed soul. With unutterable delight the children of earth enter into the joy and the wisdom of unfallen beings. They share the treasures of knowledge and understanding gained through ages upon ages in contemplation of God's handiwork. With undimmed vision they gaze upon the glory of creation—suns and stars and systems, all in their appointed order circling the throne of Deity. Upon all things, from the least to the greatest, the Creator's name is written, and in all are the riches of His power displayed.

And the years of eternity, as they roll, will bring richer and still more glorious revelations of God and of Christ.

And the years of eternity, as they roll, will bring richer and still more glorious revelations of God and of Christ. As knowledge is progressive, so will love, reverence, and happiness increase. The more men learn of God, the greater will be their admiration of His character. As Jesus opens before them the riches of redemption and the amazing achievements in the great controversy with Satan, the hearts of the ransomed thrill with more fervent devotion, and with more rapturous joy they sweep the harps of gold; and ten thousand times ten thousand and thousands of thousands of voices unite to swell the mighty chorus of praise.

"And every creature which is in heaven, and on the earth, and under the earth, and such as are in the sea, and all that are in them, heard I saying, Blessing, and honor, and glory, and power, be unto Him that sitteth upon the throne, and unto the Lamb for ever and ever." Revelation 5:13.

The great controversy is ended. Sin and sinners are no more. The entire universe is clean. One pulse of harmony and gladness beats through the vast creation. From Him who created all, flow life and light and gladness, throughout the realms of illimitable space. From the minutest atom to the greatest world, all things, animate and inanimate, in their unshadowed beauty and perfect joy, declare that God is love.